GLASS PAINTING
in an
AFTERNOON

Glass Painting
in an
Afternoon

Mickey Baskett

Sterling Publishing Co., Inc.
New York

Prolific Impressions Publication Staff

Editor: Mickey Baskett
Copy: Sylvia Carrol
Graphics: Dianne Miller, Karen Turpin
Photography: Greg Wright
Administration: Jim Baskett
Styling: Laney Crisp McClure

Acknowledgements

Mickey Baskett thanks the following for their generous contributions:

The artists who contributed their talent to this book. These individuals have been generous enough to share their talent and knowledge of painting on glass. The following talented people made this book possible: Patty Cox, Susan Fouts, Gigi Smith-Burns, Allison Stilwell

Plaid Enterprises, Inc., in Norcross, GA for their generous contribution of Apple Barrel® Gloss Paint and FolkArt® Acrylic Colors used to paint the projects in this book.

10   9   8   7   6   5   4   3   2

First paperback edition published in 2000 by
Sterling Publishing Company, Inc.
387 Park Avenue South, New York, N.Y. 10016
© 1999 by Prolific Impressions, Inc.
Distributed in Canada by Sterling Publishing
℅ Canadian Manda Group, One Atlantic Avenue, Suite 105
Toronto, Ontario, Canada M6K 3E7
Distributed in Great Britain and Europe by Cassell PLC
Wellington House, 125 Strand, London WC2R 0BB, England
Distributed in Australia by Capricorn Link (Australia) Pty Ltd.
P.O. Box 6651, Baulkham Hills, Business Centre, NSW 2153, Australia
Printed in China
All rights reserved

Sterling ISBN 0-8069-3949-4 Trade
            0-8069-2299-0 Paper

Library of Congress
Cataloging-in-Publication Data

Baskett, Mickey.
    Glass painting in an afternoon / by Mickey Baskett.
       p. cm.
    Includes index.
    ISBN 0 0069-3949-4
    1. Glass painting and staining.   2. China painting.
I Title.
TT298.B37   1999   99-18588
748.5' 028'2--dc21   CIP

CONTENTS

Brighten Your House, Brighten Your Spirits With Painted Glass & Ceramics

With today's new paint products the technique is easy and results are professional. No kiln firing is required for these easy projects. Simply paint, allow to dry, then bake at a low temperature in your home oven. What's more, your projects are usable and washable.

Imagine setting a table for company with beautiful plates and platters that you painted yourself! Or serving friends lemonade on the patio from your glass pitcher set that shines with your own artistry! Serve tea from your specially painted teapot or coffee in your cleverly painted mugs. You would never believe it's as easy as this book shows you. Place candles in painted votive holders or under a beautifully painted hurricane shade, or paint a whole ceramic lamp. Arrange flowers in a vase you painted. Painting can be done on canisters, jars, bottles for the pantry or the bath, or decorator boxes for most any room in the house.

Learn the fun and beautiful painting techniques in the pages of this book. It's an exciting and inexpensive way to express yourself, decorate your home, or make a gift for most anyone on a moment's notice. ∾

Paints

AVAILABLE TYPES &
HOW TO USE THEM ON GLASS

A variety of paint types can be chosen for painting on glass and ceramics, ranging from water-based enamels to oil paints. You can also find special effect paints such as frosts and transparent paints as well as paints which will allow you to achieve dimensional effects. Ordinary acrylics can be used as well as new formulations of acrylics that can be baked in a home oven to increase durability.

Be sure to read the label on the paints that you choose. Some paints can be baked for durability, some must be baked, and others cannot be baked. Some are dishwasher and/or microwave safe, others are not. Some are food safe, most are not. This is very important. Unless you have ascertained that the paints are food safe, do not paint surfaces that will come in contact with food. Clear glass plates can be reverse-painted on the backside and seen from the front, or they can be painted on the front and used with a clear glass liner for food. On mugs, cups, glasses, and pitchers, keep the painting at least 1/2" below the top edge if the paint is not rated food safe.

On the following pages, the general types of paint used for painting glass and ceramic projects are discussed. General color names have been given with the projects in this book because there may be several brands of each type paint, each with its own color names. The project supply lists indicate the type of paint used for that particular project. If you want to use another type of paint, read in this section about the qualities of each type before choosing an alternative. In most cases, you can substitute types without modifying the appearance of the project. ⌒

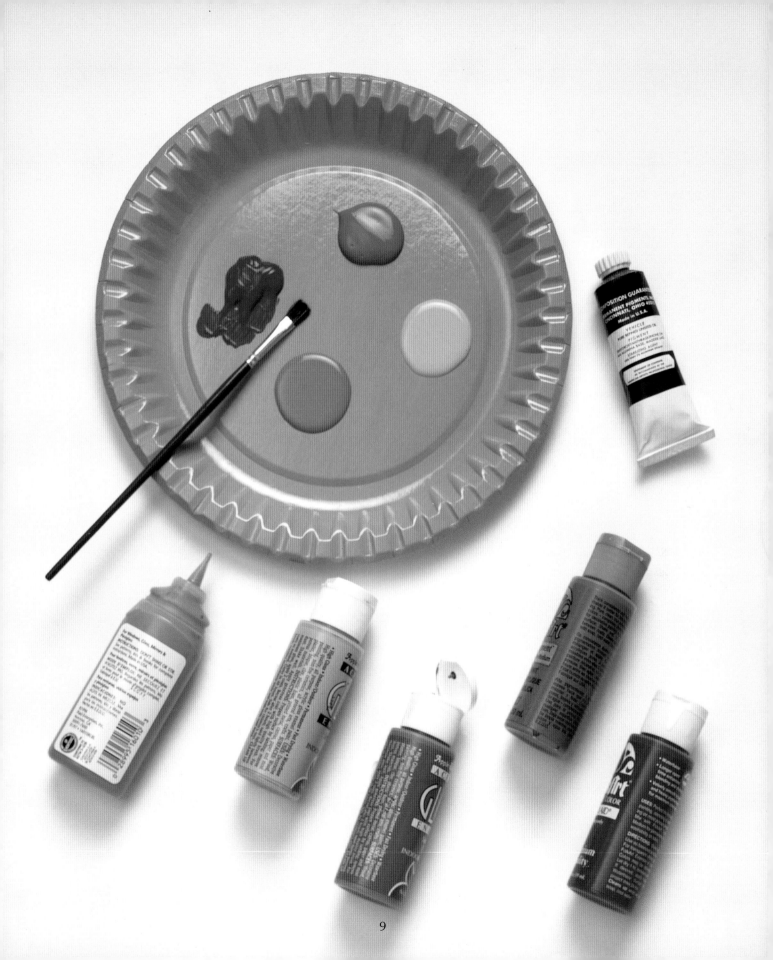

Paints

♦ OVEN-BAKE ACRYLIC ENAMELS

This type paint is one of the best choices of opaque paints when working on glass. The project is oven-baked after paint has dried for extra durability. These are water-based paints and can be thinned with water. Cleanup of brushes and spills is easy with soap or water *(if done before paint dries)*. If you make a mistake while painting, just rub or wash it away. Mistakes discovered after baking must be scraped away with a craft knife. This paint is good for sponging or stenciling as well as brush painting. Some of these type paints that are available are *not* food safe, however, check label for food safety information. The finished projects can be washed – some brands are dishwasher safe.

♦ AIR DRY ENAMEL

This is another good choice for painting on glass. Colors remain bright and glossy after air drying. These are water-based paints and can be thinned with water or a medium. Cleanup brushes and spills with soap and water. Rub or wash away mistakes while wet; scrape away with a craft knife if dry. Some brands are dishwasher and oven safe, others may not be. Check the label. This paint is good for sponging on or stenciling as well as brush painting. Check label for food safety information.

♦ AIR DRY FROSTED ENAMELS

These paints are impressive, with a very effective frosted look. This type is another excellent choice when working on glass. Do not thin this paint. Brush paint it or sponge it on. If a mistake is made, rub or wash it away, or apply another coat to cover a missed area. Cleanup is easy with soap and water. Check label for food safety information.

♦ ACRYLIC CRAFT PAINTS

Regular acrylic paints can also be used to brush paint, sponge, or stencil on glass and ceramics. These are easy to work with and there are excellent color choices. They work best when used on a matte surface. If the surface is slick, it can be given a matte finish by spraying with a matte acrylic spray. Or a glass and tile medium can be brushed on before painting, all over or only in the areas to be painted, as you desire. Thin these water based paints with water or blending medium to create a wash. For extra protection against chipping, lightly mist-spray the completed and dried painted area with at least two coats of a poly finish. Clean brushes wtih soap & water. Tube acrylics can also be used as well as the bottle acrylics. These paints are *not* food safe. Do not use on surfaces that come in contact with food. These paints are not durable on glass and should be used on only decorative items that need no washing. Dust can be removed with a damp cloth.

♦ OIL PAINTS

Oil paints adhere to glass and ceramics better than acrylics, but a protective finish is recommended. Oil paints are slow drying, but in some cases this is an advantage. It is a plus when blending colors or when wiping away areas with a texture comb. Beautiful color blends can be created on glass with oil paints. Thin this paint with mineral spirits to create a wash. If you make a mistake, carefully rub it away with mineral spirits or turpentine while wet; when dry, scrape it away with a craft knife. Oil paint sponges on well. In fact, sponged on oil paint looks better than brushed on, and thin coats look better than heavy coats. It stencils well and is somewhat superior to other paints for stamping. Clean up with mineral spirits or turpentine. Spray or paint the dried oil painting with a gloss enamel finish for a higher sheen and to protect the surface. These paints are *not* food safe. Do not use on surfaces that come in contact with food. Wash with a damp cloth, do not place in a dishwasher. These paints are best on decorative items only.

♦ GLASS STAIN PAINTS

These paints give glass the look of real stained glass. Most colors are transparent, but there are also some translucent and opaque colors. They look milky while wet, but dry to brilliant clarity. Paints can be applied directly to glass from the bottle tip. Some brands can be applied to vertical surfaces as well as horizontal ones. Do not thin these paints. Dilute the intensity of a color, if desired, by mixing it with clear paint. If a mistake is made, rub it away while wet (using a cotton swab for this works well). If dry, score the area with a craft knife and peel up the mistake; then reapply paint. These are water based paints. Clean up with soap and water. They are *not* food safe. Do not use on surfaces that come in contact with food. These paints should be used on decorative items only – they cannot be washed.

♦ AIR DRY CRYSTAL PAINTS

These paints dry similar to glass stain paints, but have a more fluid consistency. They sponge on well. Cleanup is easy with soap and water. They are *not* food safe. Do not use on surfaces that come in contact with food.

♦ AIR DRY GELS

These are also impressive. They are effective dimensional, transparent paints. Dimension can be obtained by troweling on the gel with a palette knife or dabbing it on with your finger or a brush. They can also be brush painted. In addition, the paint can be squeezed on directly from the tube. This paint adheres well to glass. If a mistake is made, just rub or wash it away while wet. Cleanup is easy with soap and water. It is *not* food safe. Do not use on surfaces that come in contact with food. ⌐

Brushes

Paint the designs with regular artist or decorative painting brushes. These include flats, shaders, rounds, angle brushes, and liners in a variety of sizes. Some projects specify both type and size of brush to use. Most projects specify the type but some may leave the size up to you. A few projects leave both the size and type up to your preference. When you choose your brush size, use the largest brush you feel comfortable with to accomodate the size design you are painting. Your goal is to fill the design area with paint in one stroke, rather than making many strokes to fill the area. Acrylics on glass tend to "lift" so it is best to use as few strokes as possible to accomplish the painting. Sable brushes are best to use with oil paints, synthetic brushes are best for acrylics.

Even the handles of our paint brushes can be useful. They are great for making dots. Simply dip the handle end into paint, then stamp it onto the surface to create a perfect dot of paint. ⁓

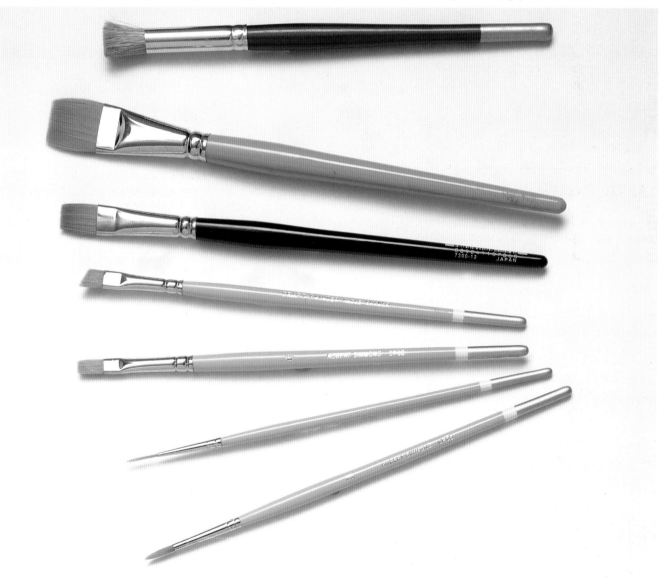

Pictured top to bottom: stencil brush, 3/4" flat brush, #12 flat shader, 1/4" angle shader, #6 flat, #00 liner, #3 round.

Surfaces to Decorate

A variety of clear glass and glazed ceramic items were used for these projects. Dishes, vases, bottles, jars, canisters, lamps, candle holders and much more are readily available and inexpensive in craft shops, outlet stores, and department stores. You can find them in secondhand stores and garage or rummage sales even more inexpensively. Blank ceramic tiles can be found at home improvement stores.

◆ GLASS

These include vases, bottles and jars, canisters, plates, pitchers, glasses, candle holders, and many other items. They may be clear or tinted, shiny or frosted, and even transparent or opaque. Glass comes in many colors. Glass items may be plain or embossed with designs or borders.

◆ GLAZED CERAMICS

Ceramic plates, canisters, vases, lamps, mugs, decorator boxes, teapots and more are easily found in a variety of colors. Most are quite inexpensive. These, too, can be plain or have embossed design elements or borders. You can find them at craft shops as well as houseware departments.

◆ TILES

Painted ceramic tiles are wonderful for decorating a wall, either as a single small accessory or as a larger tiled area. Or use them as trivets. Tiles can also line a tray or border a vanity. They are available in many colors and in a variety of sizes. ∼

Other Tools & Supplies

Many tools and supplies besides brushes can be used to apply paint or create texture or other painted effects.

Sponges: Paint can be sponged on for an overall textural look, or shaped sponges can be used to "stamp" a design. In this book, we have used a square sponge to stamp a checkerboard design.

Texture Combs: These can be found in faux finishing departments. The paint is applied to the surface and then the combing tool is pulled through the paint to create a design such as straight lines, wavy lines, or swirls.

Design Stamps: There are a wide variety of designs available in these foam-type stamps. They are soft and flexible so that they are great to use on curved surfaces of glasses, bowls, pitchers, etc. Paint is applied to the stamp surfaces, then they are pressed onto the glass surface.

Stencils: Stenciling gives you an easy option for applying a design to a surface. There are hundreds of stencil designs available in most any size needed – from simple one-overlay types to more complex types with multiple overlays. For best results on glass use the simple one-overlay type, pouncing the paint onto the glass with a brush or sponge.

Masking Tape: Masking tape can be a very valuable tool. It can mask out areas between stripes, creating clean, crisp lines, or mask over already-painted areas so that no further paint gets on your design. ∽

13

PAINTING
TECHNIQUES

On the following pages, you will learn terrific techniques for decorating glass and ceramics with paint.

• *Painting a design can be as simple as making some brush strokes and enhancing them with outlining.*

• *A textured look is achieved by sponging on the paint.*

• *Paint can be stamped on, either with a design stamp or a sponge cut to a particular shape.*

• *Texture tools such as combs can be used to create wonderful design effects in wet paint.*

There are no limits to art and imagination!

Design Painting On Glass

♦ PREPARE THE SURFACE

If there are sticky labels or grease on surface, use adhesive remover to clean off these substances. Then wipe surface thoroughly with rubbing alcohol to ensure adhesion of paint to surface. To remove surface dirt or dust, wash item first in warm sudsy water, then wipe with rubbing alcohol and a paper towel.

♦ HOW TO USE THE PATTERNS

Trace the Pattern

Trace the pattern for your project from the book onto tracing paper with a pencil or fine tip marker. Enlarge or reduce on a copier if necessary to fit your project.

Option 1: Placing the Pattern Behind the Glass

When painting on clear glass, this is the simplest method of following the design pattern. You can simply place the pattern behind the glass (under a plate, inside a vase, etc.) and tape it in place. You will be able to see the pattern through the glass. Simply follow it as you paint.

Another option is to place the pattern behind the glass and trace it onto your painting surface with a grease pencil, a crayon, or a fine tip marker (not permanent).

Option 2: Transferring the Pattern

Position the pattern in place on your project and tape to secure. The surfaces of glass and ceramic items are often curved or irregular, so it is helpful to cut excess tracing paper away from the design. Slip transfer paper between the traced pattern and the project surface, shiny side down. Use dark transfer paper if the surface is light or white transfer paper if the surface is dark. Retrace the pattern with a stylus to transfer it to your project surface.

continued on next page

Option 1: Placing the Pattern Behind the Glass.

Option 2: Transferring the Pattern.

continued from page 16

Option 3: Free-handing Design

For very simple designs, you can use the pattern simply as a visual guide as you freehand your design with a grease pencil or fine tip marker onto the surface. Or, if you are confident, you can simply begin painting directly on the surface without aid of a drawn pattern.

Option 3: Free-handing Design

◆ PAINT YOUR DESIGN

Lay out the paint colors specified on a palette. A disposable picnic plate is a good palette substitute. Have water for rinsing brushes (or mineral spirits for oil paints) and paper towels or rags handy. Follow the simple painting steps as directed in the project "here's how" section to apply the paint.

Painting Your Design

◆ BAKE OR AIR DRY PROJECTS

Some paints must be baked, others must air dry.

Air Drying: Read the label on the brand of paint you are using to determine drying time. Place your project on a level surface in a dust free area to dry.

Baking:

1. Let your piece dry for 48 hours to be sure that all layers of paint have dried.
2. Place piece in a cool oven.
3. Set oven temperature for 325-degrees F. (165-degrees C.) or the temperature directed in the instructions. Glass must heat gradually to avoid breakage, so don't put it in a hot oven; let it heat along with the oven.
4. When oven has reached 325 degrees, bake for 10 minutes (or as directed on label).
5. Then turn oven off. Let glass cool completely in oven before moving. ⌒

Brush Stroke Patterns

LINES & PLAIDS

Lines and plaids are made with a continuous brush stroke line. The width of the brush will determine the width of the line. Fill brush adequately with paint so that you can make one continous line, if possible. Mix paint with a medium or water if using acrylics so that it is not too thick or too dry and will flow better from your brush. The more medium you add, the more transparent the paint will become. Turpentine or mineral spirits can be used with oil paints. Practice this technique until you are satisfied with the results.

Pictured right: Wide stripes are a wash of blue oil paint + mineral spirits made with a flat brush. A lot of mineral spirits are used so that the paint is more transparent. Allow wide stripes to dry before adding narrow stripes. The narrow stripes are made with purple oil paint using liner brush.

OVERLAPPING "C" STROKES

To make this type of stroke, load flat brush with paint (thinned with a medium to creamy consistency) and make a c-shaped stroke. While paint is still wet, make another "C" stroke overlapping, and beside first. Continue until you have the row as long as you want. Make another row below and overlapping the first.

Pictured right: Golden yellow oil paint that has been thinned with mineral spirits.

SHORT QUICK STROKES

This technique make a pounced-paint look. Load brush with paint and simply dab it onto the surface. Overlap the next dabbing stroke. Continue until area is filled with the color you desire. When other colors are overlapped , it can create a blended look.

Pictured left: Oil paints thinned with mineral spirits are used for this example. The colors were worked from light to dark, with golden yellow to start, then red, then plum.

TWO-COLOR BLENDING

Brushes can be double loaded with two colors to create a blended look. In the example shown below, gloss enamel paint was used. Yellow paint was load into the brush. Then one side of the brush was tipped into orange. The brush was stroked on palette to blend colors before applying to glass surface.

Another blending technique that can be used is shown on the pear example. The pear was first painted with yellow gloss enamel. While the paint was still wet, orange was applied to the side of pear that you wish to shade in a "floating" technique. To "float," the brush is loaded with a medium. Then one side of brush is loaded with paint. The brush is stroked on palette to distribute color. The loaded brush is then applied to the area you wish to shade.

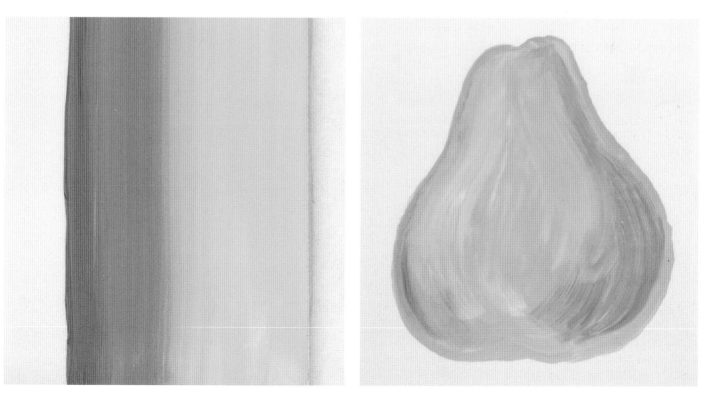

Sponging on Glass

To create a textural effect, paint can be applied with a sponge. Different effects are achieved from using a natural sea sponge versus a kitchen sponge. Project instructions will indicate when the sponge used was a sea sponge; otherwise, a kitchen or cellulose sponge was used. Always prepare sponge by first moistening with water to make it soft. Squeeze out all excess water.

Pictured right: The vase example shows overall sponging as well as reverse sponging with a stamp design.

OVERALL SPONGING

Dip the moistened sponge into the paint on palette. (A disposable plate makes a good palette for sponging.) Pounce the sponge on a clean place on the palette a time or two to evenly distribute the paint and remove excess. Then pounce it onto project. Turn the sponge in different directions as you pounce so the textural pattern of the sponge itself will not be repeated over and over. Reload the sponge with paint when needed in the same manner as you originally loaded it.

A reverse sponging effect can be achieved also. First apply a wash of paint to the surface. Using a clean, damp sponge, dab sponge onto surface to remove some of paint and create a texture.

This shows purple gloss enamel that was painted onto the surface. A clean, damp sponge was pounced onto surface to create this texture.

This shows sponging the paint onto the surface.

SPONGING A SHAPE

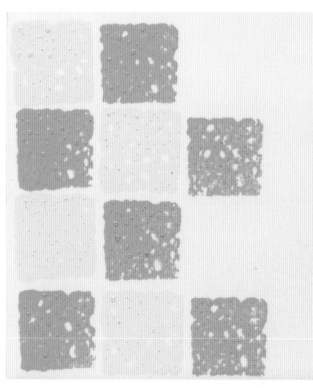

You can create a sponged shape by tracing a shape onto a kitchen sponge and cutting it out. Place the pattern on a *dry* sponge and draw around it with a fine tip pen. Cut out shape. Moisten sponge and squeeze out excess moisture. Dip it in paint and pounce on palette to distribute paint evenly. Then press the sponge shape onto your surface. You can sponge a quick checkerboard with sponge squares, or cut out more complex shapes for sponging, such as lemons or apples, crescent moons and stars, leaves, and others.

Pictured left: the examples show a checkerboard effect done with a 3/4" square sponge. Gloss enamel paints were used to sponge the squares.

21

Stamping On Glass

Another easy way to apply a painted design is to use a pre-cut stamp. Foam-type stamp designs are available in many designs at craft stores. Simply apply the paint to the stamp with a brush, a small roller, or a cosmetic sponge wedge. Blott off excess paint by stamping on a clean section of the palette first, then press the stamp to your surface. Lift stamp straight up off the surface.

After the stamped design is dry, you may wish to outline or add detailing with a liner brush. This may be for either embellishment or further definition.

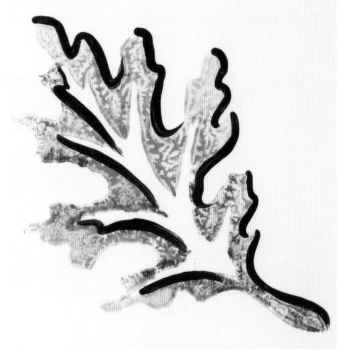

This leaf was stamped on with gloss enamel paint. After it was dry, the partial outlining was done with a liner brush and a darker color.

Stamped roses are quick and lovely. This shows the shape without any outlining.

Stamping Step-by-Step

1. Load stamp with paint, using a brush or cosmetic sponge.
2. Stamp once or twice on a clean place on your palette to remove excess paint.

3. Press stamp onto project surface.
4. Lift stamp straight up from surface.

Stenciling on Glass

Stenciling is an easy way to apply a design to a surface. There are a tremendous number of designs available – of every size and every subject matter. To stencil, simply tape the stencil to the surface of the object. Load a stencil brush or a round sponge applicator with paint. Pounce on the palette to evenly distribute paint, then pounce paint onto surface.

Other Textures

REVERSE STAMPING

In regular stamping, paint is applied with a stamp. In reverse stamping, paint is removed with a stamp. Press a clean stamp onto a wet painted area. Lift stamp straight up from surface. The paint is lifted in the design areas.

COMBING

Run a texture comb through a wet painted area to lift the paint and create a pattern. You may comb in a straight or a wavy line. For another interesting pattern, comb first in one direction, then comb across the same area in a perpendicular direction.

ENGRAVING A DESIGN

A design can be created by pulling a tool through wet paint. A toothpick, a stylus, a brush handle, or any sharp tool can be used. The area is solidly painted, then while the paint is still wet the design is drawn with the tool.

Pictured left: The design on the palm tree trunk shown in the illustration is an example of engraving. The trunk was first solidly painted. While paint was wet, a toothpick was used to draw diagonal lines.

SPATULA TEXTURE

Again, a tool was used to create a texture. The surface is first painted with a wash of paint. While wet, run a clean spatula in a wave pattern over the wash.

Pictured left: In the illustration, the wash was created with oil paint + mineral spirits.

PAINTED GLASSWARE

Plain, ordinary glass pitchers and glasses can come alive with color and style when painted on the outside. Paint with beverage themes (lemons or fruits for fruit beverages) or use colors and designs to match your other dishes or your kitchen decor. Just remember to keep the painted areas at least 1/2" below top edge if the paint you are using is not food safe.

Pictured right: Flowers & Dots Pitcher and Glasses. See project instructions on page 28.

Flowers & Dots
PITCHER AND GLASSES
Designed by Allison Stilwell

YOU WILL NEED:
Oven-Bake Acrylic Enamel Paints:
Black
Yellow
Ivory
Lavender
Violet

Item to Decorate:
Clear glass pitcher and glasses

HERE'S HOW:

Pitcher:
NOTE: Use a generous amount of paint.
1. Paint handle and base of pitcher with yellow. Let dry.
2. Decorate the yellow areas with lavender dots. Let dry.
3. Using pattern of large sunflower, transfer four around pitcher near bottom or tape pattern in place inside pitcher while painting.
4. Paint petals of sunflower with violet. Fill in centers with ivory. Let dry.
5. Decorate ivory centers with black dots.

Glasses:
1. Fill a round brush with a generous amount of yellow paint. Paint a swirly line around the base of each glass. Let dry.
2. Decorate yellow border with lavender dots.
3. Using small sunflower pattern, transfer sunflowers around glass above swirly line. Use as many as needed to go around glass. Seven are used on the glasses in the photo.
4. Paint centers with ivory. Paint petals with purple. Let dry.
5. Decorate ivory centers with black dots.

Finish:
1. Let pieces dry for 48 hours.
2. Bake the pieces as directed in "Bake or Air Dry Projects". ⌒

Actual-size Pattern – Lg. Sunflower (Pitcher)

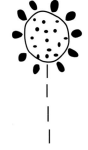

*Actual-size Pattern –
Sm. Sunflower (Glasses)*

PRETTY PLATES

Paint pretty plates for different reasons. Purely decorative plates can be displayed on the wall or set in an easel for a surface accessory. Or set a colorful and exquisite table. If you are not using food-safe paint, clear glass plates can be reverse painted on the backside and the design will show through from the front – safely and beautifully. Or, you can use the painted plate as a charger underneath a clear glass liner plate on which the food is served. It's elegant! Remember to gently hand-wash your special hand-painted plates.

Pictured right: Artichoke & Olives Decorative Plate. See project instructions on page 32.

Artichoke & Olives
DECORATIVE PLATE
Designed by Patty Cox
Pictured on page 31

YOU WILL NEED:

Oven-Bake Acrylic Enamel Paints:
Avocado green
Black
Burgundy

Item to Decorate:
Mustard-colored ceramic plate, 12" diam.

Other Supplies:
Paint brushes: flat and liner
16 amber flat-back marbles
Epoxy glue
Masking tape

HERE'S HOW:

1. Transfer artichoke pattern in center of plate. Mark eight dots evenly spaced around plate rim.
2. Paint the artichoke with avocado green. Let dry. Then float burgundy along edges of artichoke leaves as shown in the photo of project.
3. Paint an avocado green wavy line around the rim of plate with the outward curve of the wave on each of the dots.
4. Transfer leaf pattern around rim, if needed, or simply freehand the leaf with avocado green paint. A leaf goes outside the wavy line at the beginning of each outward curve and inside the wavy line at the beginning of each inward curve. Let the green paint dry. Then paint half of each leaf with burgundy.
5. Paint the backside of each amber marble with black. Let dry.
6. Remove any noticeable transfer lines with a pencil eraser; first be sure paint is dry.
7. Allow paint to dry for 48 hours. Then bake plate and the marbles and let cool as directed in "Bake or Air Dry Projects."
8. Glue "black olive" marbles to rim of plate around the wavy line with epoxy glue. Hold marbles in place with masking tape until glue dries. ∼

Actual-size Pattern for center of plate

Pattern for leaf border: repeat around rim of plate.

Sunny Day Home Plate Set
Instructions on page 34

Sunny Day Home
PLATE SET
Designed by Susan Fouts
Pictured separately on pages 36 &37

This charming set is composed of a decorative charger plate with the house design painted on the front; and a liner plate with the clouds and sun painted on the backside. There is no paint on the frontside of the liner plate so there is not a problem with placing food on this plate. When the liner plate is placed on top of the house design plate, a dimensional picture is created.

YOU WILL NEED:
Oven-Bake Acrylic Enamel Paints:
Black
Brown
Green
Red
Red-orange
Royal blue
Violet
White
Yellow

Item to Decorate:
Clear glass plate, 10" diam.
Clear glass plate, 8" diam.

Other Supplies:
Paint brushes: #3 round, #6 and #10 shaders, #10/0 liner

Patterns on page 33 and 36

HERE'S HOW:

House Design 10" Plate:
1. Tape house scene pattern to backside of plate. You can follow the pattern as you paint on front of plate.
2. Basecoat house with red. Several coats will be needed; let each coat dry before adding another. Paint windows with white. Basecoat door with red-orange; let dry. Paint heart on door with yellow. Paint roof with royal blue and chimney with violet. Let dry.
3. Paint tree trunk with brown. Basecoat tree foliage with green. Let dry. Make red dots for apples, using the handle end of a paint brush; vary sizes.
4. Paint fence with white. Shade with gray (white + a little black). Let dry.
5. Outline everything and paint door knob and pane divisions in windows with black. Use the liner brush.
6. Freehand a 2-row checkerboard around outer edge of plate with royal blue, using the #10 shader brush.

Cloud Design 8in Liner Plate:
1. This plate features reverse painting (the painting on back of plate is seen through from the front); it can therefore be used with food. Tape cloud design pattern to front (top) of plate. Paint on backside of plate, following pattern.
2. Paint sun rays with yellow and clouds with white. Let dry.
3. Outline all areas with black, using the liner brush.

Finish:
Let dry for 48 hours. Then bake and cool in oven as directed in "Bake or Air Dry Projects." ⌒

Sunny Day Home
Plate Set

Instructions on page 34

Lemon Cluster
DECORATIVE PLATE

Designed by Patty Cox

This plate would be a great decorative accessory on a kitchen shelf or in a breakfast room. Because this plate has a dimensional element on the front, it is used strictly for decoration.

YOU WILL NEED:

Acrylic Craft Paints:
Blue-black
Dusty lavender
Grayish blue
Green
Yellow
Teal
Ultramarine
Yellow-orange

Item to Decorate:
White ceramic plate, 10-1/2" diam.

Other Supplies:
Paint brushes: Round and #6 liner
Sponge
Clear casting resin
Aluminum foil
Fresh lemon
Epoxy glue
Polyurethane spray finish
Empty tuna can

HERE'S HOW:

Make Lemons:

1. Form the dimensional lemons three days in advance. Tear three 6" lengths of aluminum foil. Stack the three pieces of foil and then fold them in half (all together). Cut lemon in half lengthwise. Press foil around a lemon half to create a mold. Place mold in a tuna can, open side up to secure. (If desired, make three molds so you can cast all the lemons at once.)
2. Mix resin. Pour in lemon mold. Let dry. Make three lemon halves.

Paint Plate:

1. Mark a 5" circle in center of plate. Paint the circle with blue-black; leave areas for lemons unpainted (see photo of project). Let dry. Scratch off X's in an all-over pattern on center circle.
2. Mark a border approximately 1-1/2" wide with a scalloped outer edge around center circle. Paint border with dusty lavender. Let dry. Paint coil shapes in an all-over pattern on border with grayish blue as shown in photo of project. Let dry.
3. Using patterns, transfer and paint sets of two leaves at three equal points around outside of center circle (on circle and overlapping border – see photo of project). Paint leaves with green. Shade with teal. Highlight with yellow. When dry, outline with ultramarine + teal.
4. Using border pattern, transfer and paint leaves with same colors as larger leaves. Paint dots with the handle end of a brush. Dip it in yellow, then slide the side of dipped handle into yellow- orange. Repeat border all around edge of plate.

Add Lemons & Finish:

1. When resin lemons have dried, remove from foil molds and sponge them with yellow. Sponge on shading with yellow-orange. Let dry.
2. Glue lemons in a cluster in center of plate with epoxy glue. Refer to photo of project. Let dry.
3. Spray plate with polyurethane finish. ⌒

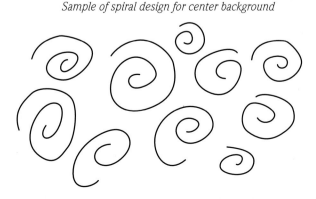

Sample of spiral design for center background

*Pattern for Border –
repeat around edge of plate*

*Pattern for Large leaves –
center section*

Funky Folk Heart

PLATE

Designed by Susan Fouts

YOU WILL NEED:

Oven-Bake Acrylic Enamel Paints:
Black
Red
Royal blue

Item to Decorate:
Clear glass plate, 10" diam.

Other Supplies:
Paint brushes: #3 round; #6 and #14
shaders

Pattern on page 43

HERE'S HOW:

1. Place pattern behind glass and tape to secure. You will be able to see the pattern through the plate as you paint.
2. Paint the heart with red.
3. Paint dots with royal blue, using the round brush.
4. Paint rickrack with red.
5. Paint checks with black, using the #14 shader.
6. Let dry for 48 hours. Then bake and cool in oven as directed in "Bake or Air Dry Projects." ⌒

Pictured left to right: Checks 'n Flowers, Funky Folk Heart, Stripes & Zigzags.

Checks 'n Flowers

LUNCHEON PLATE

This plate features reverse painting, meaning that the painting on back of plate is seen through from the front. Even if you are not using food-safe paint, this plate can be used to eat on because the painting is on the back and does not touch the food.

Pictured on page 40

YOU WILL NEED:

Oven-Bake Acrylic Enamel Paints:
Black
Green
Pink
Yellow
Royal blue
Red

Item to Decorate:
Clear textured glass luncheon plate, 8" diam.

Other Supplies:
Paint brushes: round and flat

HERE'S HOW:

1. Tape pattern to front (top) of plate. Paint on backside of plate, following pattern.
2. The checkerboard in center is composed of 5/8" squares. Alternate squares on each row with clear unpainted squares; stagger squares on next row, painting under the clear squares. Paint one horizontal row of squares with red and the next horizontal row with royal blue. Alternate colors on each row for entire center section.
3. Paint flowers in middle of rim, repeating the flower all the way around rim (17 times shown on project in the photo). Paint blossoms with pink dots and leaves with green.
4. For 1/4" wide border around outer edge, paint 1/2" black checks with approximately 1-1/2" between them. Paint spaces between black checks with yellow.
5. Let dry for 48 hours. Then bake and cool in oven as directed in "Bake or Air Dry Projects." ⌒

Stripes & Zigzags

LINER PLATE

Designed by Susan Fouts

Pictured on page 41

This plate may be used as a liner plate on top of "Funky Folk Heart" Plate which will add dimension and yet another element to the design. This plate features reverse painting, meaning that the painting on back of plate is seen through from the front. Even if you are not using food-safe paint, this plate can be used to eat on because the painting is on the back and does not touch the food.

YOU WILL NEED:

Oven-Bake Acrylic Enamel Paints:
Green
Yellow

Item to Decorate:
Clear glass plate, 8" diam.

Other Supplies:
Paint brush: #6 shader

HERE'S HOW:

1. Tape pattern in place on the front of the plate.
2. On backside of plate, paint stripes with green and zigzag or curvy lines with yellow.
3. Let dry for 48 hours. Then bake and cool in oven as directed in "Bake or Air Dry Projects." ⌒

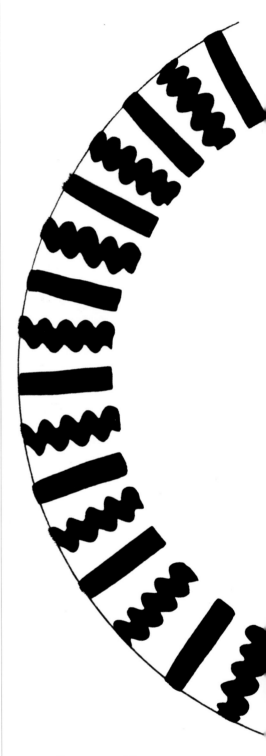

Stripes & Zigzags

Checks 'n Flowers

Pattern for 1/4 of plate. Reverse and repeat to complete design.

Funky Folk Heart

Instructions on page 40
Pattern for center of plate

Repeat flower design around plate.

Border design: repeat around rim of plate.

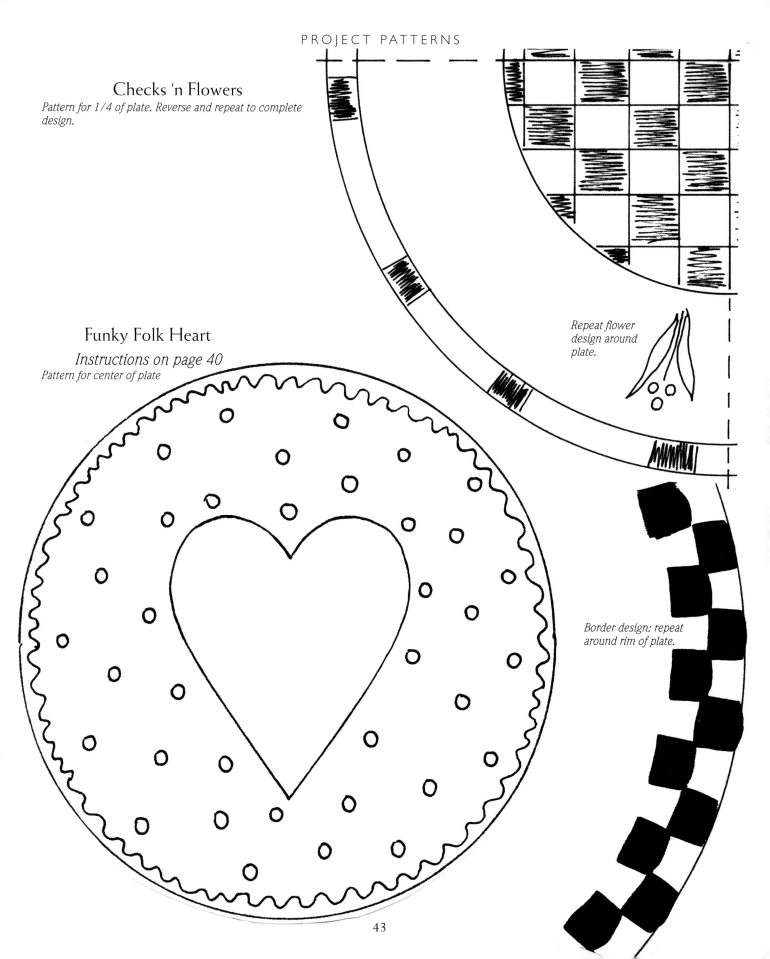

MAKE
MUGS
PERSONAL

Most of us have a favorite mug that just seems to fit us more than others. Now your favorite mug can be even more special because you hand-painted it to suit just what you like. It's also a lovely way to create a tailor-made gift for a friend, teacher, boss, or other recipient.

Remember, if you are not using food safe paint, keep your painted design 1/2" or more below the upper edge of the mug.

Pictured right: Bee Happy Mug, Happy Birdhouse Mug, and Hens 'n Chicks Mug. See instructions on pages 46 & 47.

Bee Happy
SOUP MUG
Designed by Susan Fouts
Pictured on page 45

YOU WILL NEED:

Oven-Bake Acrylic Enamel Paints:
Black
Green
Purple
Red
Red-orange
Royal blue
Violet
White
Yellow

Item to Decorate:
White soup mug

Other Supplies:
Paint brushes: #1 round, #6 shader, #10/0 liner
Graphite transfer paper

HERE'S HOW:

1. Transfer pattern to one side of mug with graphite paper.
2. Basecoat beehive with two or three coats of red-orange, letting dry after each coat. Paint stripes with a half-and-half mix of yellow + red-orange. Let dry. Outline beehive with black, using liner.
3. Paint all stems and leaves with green. Let dry. Paint veins on leaves with black, using liner.
4. Paint all flower centers with yellow. Let dry. Paint outer rings of flowers with the following colors, left to right: violet, red-orange, blue, red, purple, red-orange, red, and royal blue. Let dry. Paint a dot in center of each flower and outline left side of flower centers with black, using liner.
5. Basecoat bees' bodies with yellow. Let dry. Paint wings with white. Let dry. Paint heads, antennae, and stripes and outline bodies and wings with black, using liner.
6. Paint lettering with royal blue.
7. Let dry for 48 hours. Then bake and cool in oven as directed in "Bake or Air Dry Projects." ⌣

Happy Birdhouse
TALL MUG
Designed by Susan Fouts
Pictured on page 45

YOU WILL NEED:

Oven-Bake Acrylic Enamel Paints:
Black
Brown
Green
Red
Red-orange
Royal blue
White
Yellow

Item to Decorate:
Tall white mug

Other Supplies:
Paint brushes: #3 round, #6 shader, #10/0 liner
Graphite transfer paper

HERE'S HOW:
1. Transfer pattern to one side of mug with graphite paper.
2. Basecoat birdhouse with several generous coats of royal blue. Let dry after each coat. Basecoat roof with black. Let dry. Paint chimney with red-orange. Paint window with white, triangle border at bottom with yellow, hole with black, and perch and pole with brown. Let dry. Add detailing with black, using a liner brush.
3. Paint vine with green.
4. Paint a 2-row checkerboard board around entire bottom of mug with red, using the shader.
5. Let dry for 48 hours. Then bake and cool in oven as directed in "Bake or Air Dry Projects." ⌒

Patterns on page 48

Hens 'n Chicks
COFFEE MUG
Designed by Susan Fouts
Pictured on page 45

YOU WILL NEED:

Oven-Bake Acrylic Enamel Paints:
Black
Red
Red-orange
Royal blue
Violet
Yellow

Item to Decorate:
White ceramic mug

Other Supplies:
Paint brushes: #3 round, #6 shader, #10/0 liner
Graphite transfer paper

HERE'S HOW:
1. Transfer pattern to one side of mug with graphite paper.
2. Basecoat body of hen with several generous coats of violet. Let dry after each coat. Paint comb and wattle with red; paint beak and legs with red-orange. Paint dots on body with royal blue. Let dry. Add a red-orange dot to center of each blue dot.
3. Basecoat chicks' bodies with yellow. Paint beaks and legs with red-orange. Let dry.
4. Outline and paint all detail with black, using the liner brush.
5. Let dry for 48 hours. Then bake and cool in oven as directed in "Bake or Air Dry Projects." ⌒

Patterns on page 48

Happy Birdhouse Tall Mug
Instructions on page 47

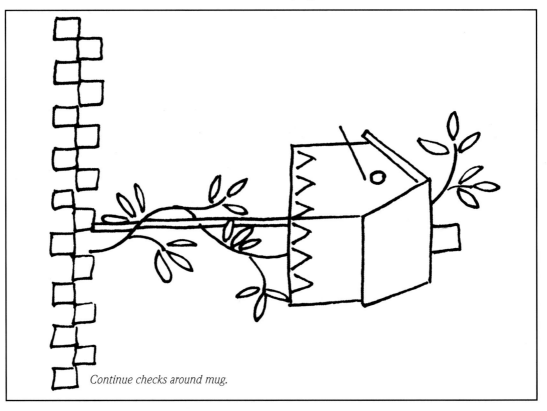

Continue checks around mug.

Hens 'n Chicks Coffee Mug

Wintry Weather Ceramic Mugs
Instructions on page 50

Pattern for Starstruck Snowman.

Pattern for Let It Snow.

Wintry Weather
CERAMIC MUGS
Designed by Susan Fouts

LET IT SNOW

YOU WILL NEED:

Oven-Bake Acrylic Enamel Paints:
Black
Red-orange
Rose
Royal blue
Yellow

Item to Decorate:
White ceramic mug

Other Supplies:
Paint brushes: #1 and #3 round
Graphite transfer paper

HERE'S HOW:

1. Transfer pattern to one side of mug with graphite paper.
2. Paint carrot nose with two or three coats of red-orange; let dry after each coat. Paint stripes on nose with a half-and-half mix of red-orange + yellow.
3. Paint spiral cheeks with rose.
4. Paint eyes and mouth with black.
5. Paint lettering with royal blue.
6. Let dry for 48 hours. Then bake and cool in oven as directed in "Bake or Air Dry Projects." ⌣

See pattern on page 49.

STARSTRUCK SNOWMAN

YOU WILL NEED:

Oven-Bake Acrylic Enamel Paints:
Black
Brown
Green
Red
Red-orange
Rose
Violet
White
Yellow

Item to Decorate:
Navy blue ceramic mug

Other Supplies:
Paint brushes: #3 round, #6 shader,
#10/0 liner
White transfer paper

HERE'S HOW:

1. Transfer design to front of mug with white transfer paper.
2. Basecoat body of snowman with several generous coats of white; let dry after each coat. Paint stick arms with brown, earmuffs with red (with white connector), cheeks with rose, carrot nose with red-orange, and eyes, mouth, and buttons with black. Basecoat scarf with green. Let dry. Paint stripes and fringe with violet. When dry, outline top of carrot and detail it with black, using a liner brush. Also outline front side of earmuffs with black.
3. Paint star with yellow. Paint string from star to arm with white.
4. Make white dots for snowflakes around design, using the handle end of a brush.
5. Let dry for 48 hours. Then bake and cool in oven as directed in "Bake or Air Dry Projects." ⌣

See pattern on page 49.

TEAPOTS & TEA CUPS

Every little girl loves a tea party. Perhaps that's why, as adults, we love serving tea in the prettiest teapots we can find. Indeed, serving tea is even worthy of ceremony worldwide. And decorating them seems to come naturally. Ceramic teapots are widely available in a variety of colors and sizes. They are just waiting for you to work your magic on them with a paint brush. Remember, if paints are not food safe, keep your painted design at least 1/2" from the tip of the spout.

Pictured right: Roses & Diamonds Teapot and Cup. See instructions on page 56.

Simple Roses
TEAPOT & CUP
Designed by Allison Stilwell

YOU WILL NEED:
Oven-Bake Acrylic Enamel Paints:
Black
Dark green
Rose

Items to Decorate:
Small white ceramic teapot
Small white ceramic cup

Other Supplies:
Paint brushes: round and fine liner
Graphite transfer paper
Fine marker (optional)

HERE'S HOW:
1. Transfer the patterns to teapot and cup with graphite paper, or draw them freehand with a marker. The roses are simply circles with simple leaf shapes. Transfer the single rose three times evenly spaced around cup.
2. With a round brush, basecoat roses with a generous amount of rose paint. Let dry.
3. With round brush, basecoat leaves with a generous amount of dark green paint. Let dry.
4. Paint the knob on the teapot lid with rose. Let dry. Add two leaves coming out from the knob with dark green. Let dry.
5. Paint outlining and detail with a liner brush and black paint. The circle becomes a rose by adding circles to the inside. Start with a small black circle and add ovals or circles around this one. You can start in the center for a rose that faces you, or start off to the side for a rose that is turned toward one side or the other. Be sure to add this detailing to the rose colored knob on top of lid to make it a rose. For leaves, add vein lines and shading lines as shown on pattern.
6. Let dry for 48 hours. Then bake and cool in oven as directed in "Bake or Air Dry Projects." ⁓

Pattern for Cup

Pattern for Teapot

Roses & Diamonds
TEAPOT & CUP
Designed by Patty Cox
Pictured on page 53

YOU WILL NEED:
Oven-Bake Acrylic Enamel Paints:
Avocado green
Burgundy
Dusty blue
Green
Light green
Light mustard
Red
Red-orange
Rose

Items to Decorate:
Moon yellow ceramic teapot, 6" high
Moon yellow ceramic mug

Other Supplies:
Paint brushes: 1/2" flat, #3 round, and #00 liner
Fine tip marker
Sponge

HERE'S HOW:
Teapot:
1. Mark dashed lines around teapot with the fine tip marker at the following levels, measuring down from the top: 1", 2", 4", 4-1/2", and 5-1/2".
2. TRIANGLES: Draw triangular points around top opening of pot, triangles measuring 3/4" wide and 1" long (down to the 1" dashed line around pot). Paint these points with dusty blue. Let dry.
3. DIAMONDS: Cut a 3/4" square from sponge. Sponge (using a stamping fashion) diamond shapes with light mustard around pot between the top dusty blue points. Bottoms of these diamonds should be along the 2" dashed line. Let dry.
4. Use the same 3/4" square sponge to do the overall sponging on the lid rim and base of teapot. Dip sponge into light mustard paint and sponge bottom of pot below the bottom (5-1/2") dashed line. Also sponge the outer rim of lid. Pounce sponge all over area, overlapping and moving sponge for an overall coverage.
5. Transfer pattern of roses around pot below the diamonds, using graphite paper (or draw 2" diameter circles). Bottoms of roses should be along the 4" dashed line. Transfer or draw three roses evenly spaced on each side of pot. Use the small rose pattern in center of lid.
6. ROSES: Dip flat brush in red-orange, then dip one side of brush in yellow and the other side in red. Basecoat roses. (If you drew circles, paint them in with a scalloped edge.) Dip flat brush in rose, then dip one side in yellow and the other side in red-orange. Continue painting a scalloped pattern on rose area. Continue painting more scallops on the rose areas, alternating red-orange, rose, yellow, and red until there is a mottling of colors on the rose. Let dry. Outline rose petal areas with burgundy.
7. LEAVES: Paint top of each leaf with light green and bottom of each leaf with avocado green.
8. At the 4-1/2" marked line below roses, make short brush strokes all around pot using disty blue and a 1/2" flat brush.
9. STRIPES: Paint vertical stripes with rose, spaced 1/2" apart, on light mustard sponged section at bottom of pot and around edge of lid. Use the #3 round brush to make stripes.
10. Use the handle end of a brush dipped into dusty blue to make little dots all along the top of the sponged area at bottom of pot.

Cup:
1. Measure and mark lines around cup at 1/2" and 1" down from upper edge.
2. TRIANGLES: Draw a border of triangles between these lines, making tops of triangles 3/4" wide. Points should reach bottom of the two lines. Paint triangle border with dusty blue.
3. ROSES: Transfer pattern of small rose to each side of cup below triangle border with graphite paper (or simply mark 1-1/2" circles where roses should go). Paint roses as directed for teapot.
4. Around bottom of cup below roses, stamp a diamond border with the 3/4" square sponge dipped in light mustard paint.

Finish:
1. Remove all noticeable pen lines with a pencil eraser.
2. Let dry for 48 hours. Then bake and cool in oven as directed in "Bake or Air Dry Projects."

Pattern for large rose – repeat 6 times around teapot.

Pattern for small rose – place on teapot lid & cup.

Starry Night
Votive Holder
Instructions on page 65

Tulip Impressions Lamp
Instructions on page 60
Pattern for lamp base – repeat around.

LAMPS
AND
LIGHTS

Light adds an extra dimension to your painted projects, whether it shines through from inside or spotlights from above. These projects include a lamp and shade, hurricane cover, and a variety of votive candle holders.

Lamps with ceramic bases abound and are inexpensive. You may even have an old one on hand that needs a new look. Glass hurricane shades or chimneys come in a variety of sizes and shapes and in transparent and frosted glass. There's no end to the variety of votive candle holders. Some especially nice effects can be created with them by gluing on flat-back marbles as part of the design or leaving unpainted shapes for the light to shine through. Remember, be safe, don't leave your candles unattended.

Pictured right: Tulip Impressions Lamp Shade & Base. See project instructions on page 60.

Tulip Impressions
LAMP & SHADE
Designed by Patty Cox
Pictured on page 59

YOU WILL NEED:
Air Dry Enamel Paints:
Apple green
Black
Dark blue-green
Fuchsia
Light green
Metallic gold
Red
Red-orange
Yellow

Items to Decorate:
White ceramic ginger jar lamp base, 6-1/2" high
White lampshade, 4" top diam. x 10" bottom diam. x 7" high

Other Supplies:
Paint brushes: 1/2" flat, #3 round, and #00 liner
Crackle medium
Sponge
Polyurethane spray finish
Graphite transfer paper
Steel wool
Patterns are on page 57 & 61.

HERE'S HOW:

Lamp Base:
1. Thoroughly clean lamp base. Scuff surface with steel wool.
2. Transfer pattern to lamp base with graphite paper. Leave 3/4" at bottom below pattern.
3. Apply a generous amount of crackle medium to lamp base. Let dry. You should be able to see pattern through the crackle medium when dry. Cracks will form as you add your painted design.
4. BACKGROUND: Paint the background yellow around tulips and leaves, including the 1/2" space at bottom. Add short strokes of metallic gold on the yellow background. Let dry.
5. TULIPS: Paint tulips in a mottled fashion with fuchsia, red, yellow, and red-orange, brushing these colors on in a slip-slap fashion. Let dry.
6. LEAVES: Paint leaves with apple green and light green in long vertical strokes, placing colors in an irregular freeform manner, but still with light green basically on one side and apple green on the other side. Using the flat brush, add shading to leaves with dark blue-green in an irregular manner. Let dry.
7. Using a flat brush, add metallic gold highlights on leaves and tulips.
8. Outline tulips and leaves with black, using a liner brush.
9. STRIPES: With a flat brush, paint black vertical stripes around lamp base in the bottom 3/4" area. Leave a brush width between the stripes. With a liner brush, paint a horizontal black line around the lamp at top of stripes (top of the 1/2" area).

Lampshade:
1. Sponge the entire outside of shade with yellow. Let dry.
2. Lightly mark a line around shade 1/4" down from top edge and another at 4-3/4" down from top edge (or 2-1/2" up from bottom edge). With a clean sponge, sponge between these lines with metallic gold. Let dry.
3. VINE: In the bottom 2-1/2" yellow area, paint a wavy line for a vine with light green (see Fig. 1). Paint short stems coming out from this wavy vine line. Shade the vine line with dark blue-green. Let dry.
4. FLOWERS: Cut a 1/2" circle from sponge. Dip sponge into all tulip colors (fuchsia, red, yellow, and red-orange). At the end of each short stem, stamp one, two, or three berries with the sponge. Let dry. Highlight each berry with a metallic gold dot or short stroke.
5. TRIANGLE BORDER: Cut a 1/2" triangle from sponge. Dip sponge in black paint and stamp triangles side by side for a border (pointing upward) along bottom of gold sponged area. Let dry.
6. STRIPES: Dip flat brush in black paint. Paint vertical stripes in the 1/2" area at top edge of shade. Leave spaces the width of the brush between stripes.
7. SWIRLS: Paint yellow swirls in an all-over pattern on gold sponged area. Refer to photo of project. Let dry.
8. LETTERING: Using patterns and a liner brush, paint black lettering (LE FLEURS) in an all-over pattern between swirls. Refer to photo.

Finish:
When dry, spray lamp and shade with polyurethane finish. ⌒

Fig. 1 – To use as a pattern, trace and repeat all around lampshade.

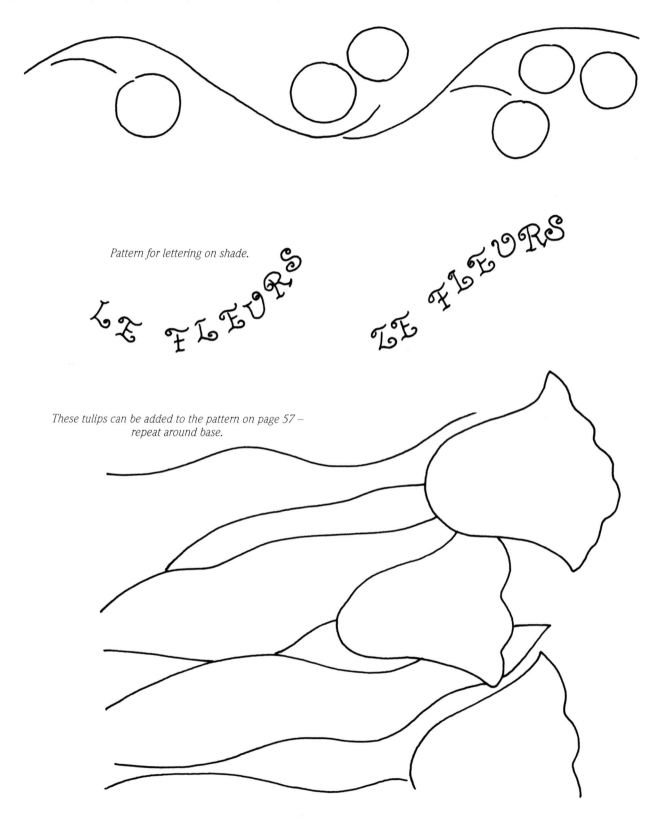

Pattern for lettering on shade.

These tulips can be added to the pattern on page 57 – repeat around base.

Field of Funky Flowers
HURRICANE SHADE & PLATE
Designed by Allison Stilwell

YOU WILL NEED:
Air Dry Enamel Paints:
Black (optional: also a black enamel
accent liner)
Dusty pink
Light green
Light plum
Violet
White (or use a white enamel accent
liner)

Item to Decorate:
Clear glass hurricane shade, 10-1/4" tall
Clear glass plate, 9" diam.

Other Supplies:
Paint brushes: 1/2" flat, 1/4" flat, and
liner (optional)

HERE'S HOW:
1. With a flat brush, paint a 1/2" border of black around top and bottom of hurricane shade and around outer rim of plate. Let dry.
2. Add a 1" line of dusty pink inside the black borders (on hurricane shade and plate). Let dry.
3. With a small brush handle and white (or with a white enamel accent liner) add white dots on the black borders.
4. Add a triangular border with light green on top of the dusty pink borders on hurricane shade, starting next to the black areas. Let dry.
5. Tape the pattern inside hurricane globe. Paint the various rings and centers of the flowers with dusty pink, light plum, violet, and light green. Refer to photo of project for color placement or use your own combinations. Let dry.
6. Use a liner brush and black paint (or a black enamel accent liner) to outline the rings of the flowers and to draw stems and leaves. Refer to photo of project. ⌣

Pattern for hurricane shade.

CRYSTAL BALL OF LIGHT

YOU WILL NEED:
Paints:
White frost

Item to Decorate:
Clear glass round votive vase, 5" diam.

Other Supplies:
26 clear glass flat-back marbles, 1/2" diam.
Paint brush: #6 flat   Small sponge
Toothpick   Masking tape
Epoxy glue   Pie tin   Plastic container

HERE'S HOW:
1. CRACK MARBLES: Preheat oven to 400 degrees. Place marbles in a pie tin. Bake in oven 25 minutes. Prepare a plastic container of ice water (with ice). Remove marbles from oven. Immediately dump marbles into ice water. In a few seconds, when cracking sound has stopped, remove marbles from water. Place on a towel to dry.
2. GLUE MARBLES around votive vase with epoxy glue. Hold each in place with masking tape until glue dries.
3. PAINT OUTSIDE OF VASE with white frost paint, using a #6 flat brush. Paint around each marble. Let dry. Optional: Apply a second coat of white frost paint with a sponge. ⌒

LATTICE & FLOWERS

YOU WILL NEED:
Air Dry Enamel Paints:
Blue   Green   Pink   White

Item to Decorate:
Square clear glass votive candle holder, 2-3/4" square x 3" high

Other Supplies:
Paint brushes: round

HERE'S HOW:
1. Measure and mark 1-1/4" down from top edge.
2. Paint a pink line around votive on marked line. Paint top rim with pink. Let dry.
3. Paint a blue lattice design below pink line. Refer to photo of project. Let dry. Make a pink dot in each lattice diamond shape, using the handle end of a brush.
4. In top area between pink line and pink rim, make simple flowers that are just a dot for flower, a line for stem, and a stroke on each side for leaves. Make flowers pink and stems and leaves green. Place four flowers on each side of votive. Let dry. Paint a wavy white line along bottom of flowers. ⌒

STARRY NIGHT
Designed by Patty Cox

YOU WILL NEED:
Oven-Bake Acrylic Enamel Paints:
Navy   Purple   Royal blue

Item to Decorate:
Clear glass round votive vase, 5" diam.

Other Supplies:
Paint brushes: round and liner   Fine tip marker
See pattern on page 57

HERE'S HOW:
1. With the fine tip marker, draw stars, moons, sunbursts, and coils on votive vase in an all-over design. The pattern gives one size of each. Feel free to vary the sizes.
2. Dip brush in purple. Paint a generous stroke of paint around one of the drawn shapes. Dip brush in royal blue. Stroke paint around another shape. Dip brush in navy. Continue stroking paint around all the drawn shapes and on background, allowing colors to blend and bleed together. ∽

MILLEFIORI SPLENDOR
Designed by Patty Cox

YOU WILL NEED:
Glass Staining Paint:
Use a variety of colors, 3 colors per floral spot, such as:
Red   Royal blue   Yellow   Green
Orange   Turquoise   Translucent white
Translucent ivory   Translucent peach
Any other colors of your choice

Item to Decorate:
Clear glass round votive vase, 4" diam.

Other Supplies:
Plastic or glass work surface   Toothpick

HERE'S HOW:
1. MILLEFIORI SPOTS: Make Millefiori spots separately on a plastic or glass work surface as follows. Make a paint dot on work surface. Apply paint directly from bottle tip. Draw a paint circle around the first color with a different color; alternate light and dark colors. Draw a paint circle around the second circle, creating a bull's eye. See Fig 1. While wet, drag a toothpick from the center color to the outer color (Fig. 2). Wipe paint off tip of toothpick with a rag. Repeat, dragging toothpick through colors six to eight times around the circle. Wipe toothpick after making each ray of the starburst. Let dry.
2. DECORATE VASE: Peel up spots from work surface one at a time. Place each on votive and rub over spot with your thumb. The spots will adhere to glass. Cover entire outside of vase. ∽

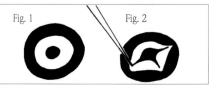
Fig. 1   Fig. 2

TERRIFIC TILES

Plain white ceramic tiles from a home improvement store are just begging for you to paint a beautiful design on them. They are a ceramic version of the artist's blank canvas. Turn these ordinary tiles into works of art and use them as trivets, for decorations on the wall, to line a tray, or for house numbers or signs. Ceramic tiles come in a variety of colors and sizes.

The projects here include a trivet tile that can be displayed on an easel when not in use and two tile sets. One set is mounted in wooden tile frame.

With tiles and a little paint, you'll never be at a loss for a gift idea.

Pictured right: Splash of Flowers Trivet Tile. See project instructions on page 68.

Splash of Flowers
TRIVET TILE

Designed by Patty Cox

Pictured on page 67

YOU WILL NEED:
Air Dry Enamel Paints:
Apple Green
Black
Lavender
Red
Rose
Teal
Yellow

Item to Decorate:
White square ceramic tile, 6"

Other Supplies:
Paint brushes: round and liner
Transfer paper

HERE'S HOW:
1. Transfer pattern onto tile.
2. Paint design, leaving white spaces between all colors. Refer to photo of project for color placement. Mix yellow + red for orange; mix apple green + yellow for light green. Let dry.
3. Outline flowers and leaves and paint border with black, using a liner brush. ∼

Pattern for trivet tile.

Bon Appetit Tile Set
Instructions on page 70

Pattern for vegetable tile and bon appetit tile.

Bon Appetit

TILE SET
Designed by Patty Cox

You Will Need:
Oven-Bake Acrylic Enamel Paints:

Avocado green	Black	Brown
Burgundy	Fuchsia	Ivory
Lavender	Mustard	Purple

Items to Decorate:
Three pale yellow square ceramic tiles, 4-1/4"
Wood tile holder (optional)

Other Supplies:
Paint brushes: flat and liner
Transfer paper

Here's How:
1. Transfer designs onto tiles.

Chef Tile:
1. Paint face with a mix of ivory + mustard + brown. Shade by adding more brown to the mix. Paint cheeks with a wash of fuchsia + ivory.
2. Paint hat with ivory. Shade with a wash of mustard. Paint coat with a wash of mustard. When dry, outline chef with brown + black, using the liner brush.
3. Paint olives with black. Paint shadows cast by olives with mustard.
4. Paint dark side of leaves with avocado green. Paint light side with avocado green + ivory. Paint shadows cast by leaves with mustard.
5. Paint olive oil bottle with purple, burgundy, and ivory. Do not mix colors. Dip brush in individual paint puddles and mottle colors with brush strokes to achieve an impressionistic look. Paint bottle label with a wash of avocado green.
6. Add a wash of purple + burgundy in top left background.
7. Paint checks around edge with avocado green flat brush strokes.

Vegetable Tile:
1. Paint avocado with a avocado green + ivory. Refer to photo of project for light and dark areas. Paint seed with mustard + ivory + brown.
2. Paint eggplant with purple + burgundy. Highlight with ivory + lavender. Paint stem with a wash of avocado green; shade it

with a brown wash; highlight it with a mustard wash.
3. Paint olives with black.
4. Paint the dark side of leaves with avocado green. Paint the light side of leaves with avocado green + ivory.
5. Paint garlic with a mustard wash. Highlight with an ivory wash. Shade with a lavender wash. Outline garlic with brown.
6. Paint the shadows cast by vegetables and leaves with a wash of mustard.
7. Paint checks around edge with avocado green flat brush strokes.

Bon Appetit Tile:
1. Paint olives with black.
2. Paint the dark side of leaves with avocado green. Paint the light side of leaves with avocado green + ivory.
3. Paint fork with purple, burgundy, and ivory. Do not mix the colors. Dip brush in individ-

ual paint colors and mottle colors with brush strokes on tile to achieve an impressionistic look.
4. Paint spoon with mustard.
5. Paint the shadows cast by vegetables, leaves, and utensils with a wash of mustard.
6. Add a purple + burgundy wash in the top right corner.
7. Paint lettering with black.
8. Paint checks around edge with avocado green flat brush strokes.

Finish:
1. When paint is dry, remove any noticeable transfer lines.
2. Let dry for 48 hours. Then bake and cool in oven as directed in "Bake or Air Dry Projects."
3. Optional: Glue tiles into wood tile frame.

Additional patterns on page 69.

Fruit A'plenty
TILE SET
Designed by Patty Cox

This set can be used in your kitchen behind your stove or sink.
It's fun to design your own tiles for your decor.

YOU WILL NEED:
Oven-Bake Acrylic Enamel Paints:
Black   Blue-black   Green
Ivory   Light plum   Medium blue
Purple   Red   Red-orange   Yellow

Items to Decorate:
Five white square ceramic tiles, 4-1/4"

Other Supplies:
Paint brushes: Flat and liner
Transfer paper

HERE'S HOW:
1. Transfer the designs onto tiles.

Plum Tile:
1. Paint plum with purple. Highlight with ivory strokes.
2. Paint leaves with yellow + green.
3. Paint background with yellow and red-orange. Do not mix colors. Dip brush in individual paint colors and mottle colors as you paint brush strokes on tiles to achieve an impressionistic look.
4. Paint outer border with medium blue + light plum.
5. Paint zigzag lines along inside of border with red-orange, light plum, and black (outside toward inside).
6. Outline plum and leaves with black.

Strawberry Tile:
1. Paint strawberry with red. Highlight with red-orange.
2. Paint bracts with yellow + green.
3. Paint background with yellow and red-orange. Do not mix colors. Dip brush in individual paint colors and mottle colors as you paint brush strokes on tiles to achieve an impressionistic look.
4. Paint outer border with blue-black.
5. Paint zigzag lines along inside of border with light plum and black (outside toward inside).
6. Outline strawberry and bracts with black.

Grapes Tile:
1. Paint grapes with green + yellow. Shade with green. Highlight with yellow.
2. Paint leaves with green and purple, mottling the colors with brush strokes.
3. Paint background with red-orange.
4. Paint outer border with blue-black..
5. Paint zigzag lines along inside of border with medium blue + light plum, light plum, and black (outside toward inside).
6. Outline grapes and leaves with black.

continued on page 74

72

continued from page 72

Peach Tile:

1. Paint peach with yellow + red-orange. Highlight with yellow. Shade with red-orange.
2. Paint leaves with yellow + green.
3. Paint background with blue-black.
4. Paint outer border with medium blue + light plum.
5. Paint zigzag lines along inside of border with black, red-orange, and light plum (outside toward inside).
6. Outline peach and leaves with black.

Pear Tile:

1. Paint pear with yellow + red-orange. Highlight with yellow. Shade with red-orange.
2. Paint leaves with yellow + green.
3. Paint background with blue-black.
4. Paint outer border with medium blue + light plum.
5. Paint zigzag lines along inside of border with black, light plum, and red-orange (outside toward inside).
6. Outline pear and leaves with black.

VASE
VARIETY

Vases come in all manner of shapes and sizes and in both glass and ceramics. They can be transparent, translucent, or opaque. They can hold a huge bouquet, a single bud, or nothing at all and still be lovely.

This collection of vases reflects a wide range of types and uses a variety of paint types. You'll find one that's meant for you. You'll also learn some exciting techniques for decorating them.

Pictured right: Floral Dimensions Flower Vase. See instructions on page 78.

Floral Dimensions

FLOWER VASE

Designed by Patty Cox

Pictured on page 77

YOU WILL NEED:

Air Dry Enamel Paints:
Apple green
Black
Dark purple
Light plum
Rose
Teal
Violet
White
Yellow

Air Dry Frosted Enamel Paints:
Lavender frost
Violet frost
White frost

Item to Decorate:
Clear glass vase, 8" high

Other Supplies:
Paint brushes: flat and liner
Sponge
16 clear glass flat-back marbles
Crayon or fine tip marker
Epoxy glue
Masking tape

HERE'S HOW:

1. Measuring up from bottom, mark lines around vase at the following levels: 2-1/2", 5- 1/2", and 6-1/2".
2. Sponge top section of vase (above the 6-1/2" line) with lavender frost. Let dry.
3. Sponge lower portion of vase (below the 2-1/2" line) with white opaque. Let dry.
4. Sponge center section (between the 2-1/2" and 5-1/2" lines) *on the inside of vase* with white frost.
5. Between the lavender frost and white frost sections (between the 5-1/2" and 6-1/2" lines), place 3/8" strips of masking tape vertically, spaced 1-1/2" apart. Sponge over taped area (between lavender frost and white frost sections) with teal. Let dry.
6. Remove masking tape. Paint light plum vertical stripes on each side of each teal sponged section. Paint vertical wavy lines with white on each side of teal sponged area *on* the teal areas (refer to photo of project). Paint a dark purple horizontal wavy line around vase at top of the teal sponged area (on the 6-1/2" line). Paint a violet horizontal wavy line around bottom of this section (on the 5-1/2" line).
7. Make dark purple dots in an all-over pattern on the top lavender frost area, using the handle end of a paint brush.
8. Cut four sponge squares, decreasing in size from 1/2" to 3/8". Sponge black squares in a 4-row checkerboard pattern over lower white section. Begin with the largest square at the top and decrease to the smallest square for the bottom row (above bottom rim of base). Then, using one of the larger squares, sponge black checks around bottom rim of base. Refer to photo of project.
9. Paint a light plum wavy line around vase between checkerboard and lower rim of vase, using a liner brush. Make dark purple dots above and below the wavy line, using the handle end of a paint brush.
10. Make a line of teal dots above checkerboard (on the 2-1/2" line), using the handle end of a paint brush.
11. Paint a yellow dot on the center backside (flat side) of each clear marble. Let dry. Paint back of each marble with rose. Let dry.
12. Mix epoxy glue with a toothpick. Apply glue to back of each marble. Position marble in white frost section of vase. Hold in place with masking tape until glue dries. Apply marbles in an all-over pattern on white frost section.
13. Paint a green leaf on each side of each marble-flower. Make white dots in an all-over pattern on background of white frost section *on outside*, using the handle end of a paint brush. ⌒

Striped Elegance
VASE
Designed by Patty Cox

YOU WILL NEED:

Air Dry Liquid Crystal Paint or Glass Stain Paint:
Amber

Item to Decorate:
Clear glass vase, 8" high

Other Supplies:
Sea sponge
Masking tape, 1/4" wide
Amber satin roping with a tassel at each end

HERE'S HOW:

1. Turn vase upside down. Tear a long strip of masking tape. Align center of tape with center bottom of vase. Tape across bottom and up each side to top of vase in a straight line (Fig. 1). Repeat with another piece of tape perpendicular to the first.

2. Add two more strips of tape in the same manner, dividing the vase into eighths (Fig. 2). Add more strips of tape, dividing the vase into sixteenths (Fig. 3).

3. Sponge vase with amber paint. Let dry. Remove tape.

4. Tie amber roping with tassels around neck of vase. Refer to photo of project.

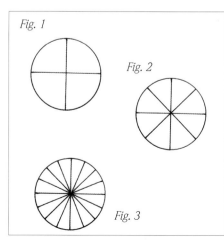

Fig. 1

Fig. 2

Fig. 3

Sea Wonders

VASE

Designed by Patty Cox

YOU WILL NEED:

Air Dry Enamel Paints:
Apple Green
Coral
Dark blue
Dark green
Indigo
Light plum
Red
Teal
Yellow

Transparent Air Dry Gel Paint or Glass Stain Paint:
Sapphire

Air Dry Frosted Enamel Paints:
Teal frost

Item to Decorate:
Clear glass vase, 7" high

Other Supplies:
Paint brushes: 1/2" flat, #3 round, and #00 liner
Eight turquoise flat-back marbles
Crayon
Epoxy glue
Masking tape

HERE'S HOW:

1. Paint the marbles with teal frost paint. Set aside.

2. Mark horizontal lines on vase with a crayon at the following levels: 2-1/2" down from top edge and 1-1/2" up from bottom.

3. Squeeze a small puddle of sapphire gel or glass stain paint on top section of vase (above upper line). With your finger, tap paint around top section. Let dry.

4. Paint a coral wavy line with a liner brush below this sapphire area. Paint another coral wavy line at the line that is 1-1/2" up from bottom.

5. Cut out and tape patterns of fish and sand dollar designs in place inside vase, between the wavy lines. Trace them on outside of vase with a crayon. Paint the designs, referring to photo of project for color placement. Outline each with a darker shade of it's own color (outline apple green with dark green, coral with red, and light plum with indigo, and teal with dark blue).

6. Paint triangles of various colors in the background of this section (between coral wavy lines), and shade each on two sides with the darker color as with the fish and sand dollars.(Shade yellow triangles with red.)

7. Paint a light plum wavy line below the bottom coral wavy line.

8. Paint apple green vertical stripes around lower portion of vase with a flat brush (stripes are the width of the brush); leave approximately 3/4" between them. Paint a teal stripe with a liner brush on each side of each apple green stripe.

9. Mix epoxy glue. Glue marbles around vase top just above the upper coral wavy line. Hold marbles in place with masking tape until glue dries. ∾

Patterns for vase

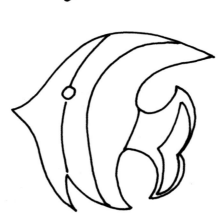

Tropical Touch
CERAMIC VASE
Designed by Patty Cox

YOU WILL NEED:
Oven-Bake Acrylic Enamel Paints:
Avocado green
Black
Burgundy

Item to Decorate:
Mustard color ceramic vase, 7" high

Other Supplies:
Paint brushes: flat and liner
Three amber flat-back marbles, approx.
1/2" wide
Sponge
Fine tip marker
Epoxy glue
Toothpick
Masking tape
Hole punch
Graphite transfer paper

HERE'S HOW:
1. Cut the following from sponge: Cut a diamond shape 1/4" x 1/2". Create a small circle from sponge by punching a dot from sponge with a hole punch.
2. Using diamond shape sponge, sponge a border of black diamonds around vase neck at 1" down from top edge.
3. Paint a burgundy wavy line around vase neck 1/2" below diamond border. Use a liner brush.
4. Paint a border of avocado green X's around neck of vase 3/8" below wavy line. Use a liner brush.

5. Paint a black wavy line around approximately 1/2" above very bottom of vase.
6. Using the dot sponge, sponge avocado green dots around vase above the black wavy line. Let dry.
7. Transfer the palm tree design. Paint the trunk with burgundy. While paint is still wet, draw X's down truck with a toothpick, lifting the paint. Refer to "Engraving a Design" in the section on "Other Textures." To complete the palm trunk texture, paint side points on trunk with a liner brush. Paint palm fronds with avocado green. Let dry. Outline fronds with black, using a liner brush.
8. Paint backsides (flat sides) of marbles with burgundy. Let dry.
9. When all paint is dry, remove any noticeable transfer lines with a pencil eraser.
10. Let vase and marbles dry for 48 hours. Then bake and cool them in oven as directed in "Bake or Air Dry Projects."
11. Mix epoxy glue. Apply glue to flat side of each marble. Glue marbles on palm tree as shown in photo of project. Hold them in place with masking tape until dry. ⌒

Pattern for palm tree.

82

Swirls of Color
ROUND VASE
Designed by Patty Cox

YOU WILL NEED:

Oil Paints:
Black
Red
Plum
Purple
Yellow-orange

Item to Decorate:
Clear glass round fish bowl type vase, 11"
diam.

Other Supplies:
Paint brush
Cotton swabs
Butterfly design stamp
Texture comb
Square kitchen sponge, approx. 1" to 1-
1/2"
Mineral spirits

HERE'S HOW:

1. Thin plum oil paint with mineral spirits to an easy brushing consistency. Brush a big "S" shape on side of vase. Brush the "S" wider at some curves and more narrow at others. (See Fig. 2)
2. Thin red oil paint. Brush another "S" shape to the left of the first, overlapping the edge of the plum area. (See Fig. 2)
3. Thin yellow-orange oil paint. Brush another "S" shape to the left of the red area, overlapping edge of red area. (See Fig. 2)
4. Moisten the square kitchen sponge with just enough water to soften the sponge. Starting on the left edge of the orange-yellow area, sponge over paint to soften strokes. Work each stroke from top to bottom, gradually moving to the right and to the darker colors. (See Fig. 3)
5. Paint and sponge two more sets of "S" shapes until you have three sets fairly evenly spaced around the vase. Allow unpainted areas between the sets of color.
6. Draw a wavy coil rose (see Fig. 1) in the wet paint with a cotton swab – one or two coils in each set of colors. Go over the lines with another swab to lift the paint.
7. Run the texture comb in a wavy line in the wet paint on one or two of the colored sections. (See Fig. 5)
8. Thin purple oil paint with mineral spirits. Brush paint in the areas between the "S" shaped colored sections. Butt two purple sections up next to another color. Leave spaces between colors on each side of the third purple area.
9. Paint a wide black line over the spaces left on each side of the third purple area. Use a stick or the handle end of a paint brush to scrape a spiral within these black borders, lifting the paint from the black line. Refer to photo of project.
10. Press a clean butterfly design stamp into the sponged paint. The stamp will lift paint, leaving an impression (See Fig. 4). Create a butterfly three times around the vase, once in each of two purple areas and once overlapping a purple and plum area.
11. Run the texture comb in a wave pattern in one of the purple areas, lifting the wet paint. ∿

See page 86 for examples of the techniques used in this project.

Fig. 1

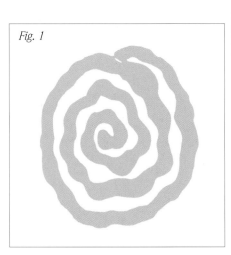

SWIRLS OF COLOR – TECHNIQUES

Fig. 2
Paint three curved lines, overlapping colors at edge of paint strokes. Plum, red, yellow.

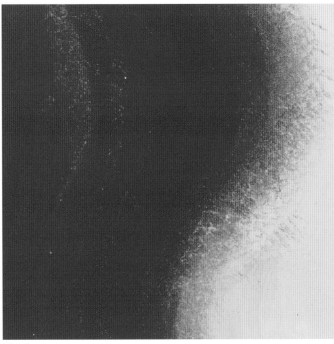

Fig. 3
Starting on right yellow edge of brush strokes, sponge over paint to soften strokes. Work each stroke from top to bottom and gradually move to the left and to the darker colors.

Fig. 4
Use a butterfly design stamp. Stamp in sponged paint. The stamp will lift paint, leaving an impression.

Fig. 5
Run texture comb in wave patterns, lifting wet paint.

Blossoms & Spiral
BUD VASE
Designed by Patty Cox

YOU WILL NEED:
The following variety of paints:
Crystal color Air Dry Gel
Indigo oil paint
Fuchsia oil paint
Gold liquid leaf paint

Item to Decorate:
Pale pink glass bud vase with long neck,
7" high

Other Supplies:
Paint brush: flat
Petal shape stamp
Sponge

HERE'S HOW:

1. Squeeze crystal gel in a spiral around neck of vase. Turn vase slowly while maintaining an even flow of gel. Let dry.

2. Paint petal stamp with fuchsia. Add a small stroke of gold leafing paint. Add a small indigo brushstroke on pointed end of petal stamp. Stamp on bottom round section of vase for petal. Stamp about three petals before reloading stamp with paint. Stamp five petals on each flower. Stamp six flowers around bottom round area of vase.

3. Paint some leaves for each flower with indigo. Highlight leaves with gold leafing paint.

4. Stipple flower centers with gold leafing paint.

5. Sponge a little gold leafing paint and fuchsia oil paint on the gel spiral around neck of vase. ～

Swirls & Marbles
Round Vase

You Will Need:
Air Dry Acrylic Paints:
White frost

Item to Decorate:
Clear glass round vase, approx. 8-1/2"
diam/ x 6-1/2" high

Other Supplies:
Paint brush: 1/4" flat
31 flat-back marbles: green, turquoise, rose,
clear
Epoxy glue
Masking tape

Here's How:
1. Paint 31 swirls approximately 2" diameter in an all-over pattern on vase. Refer to photo of project. Let dry.
2. Mix epoxy glue. Put glue on backside (flat side) of marbles. Glue a marble to center of each swirl, varying colors. Hold in place with masking tape until glue is dry. ∼

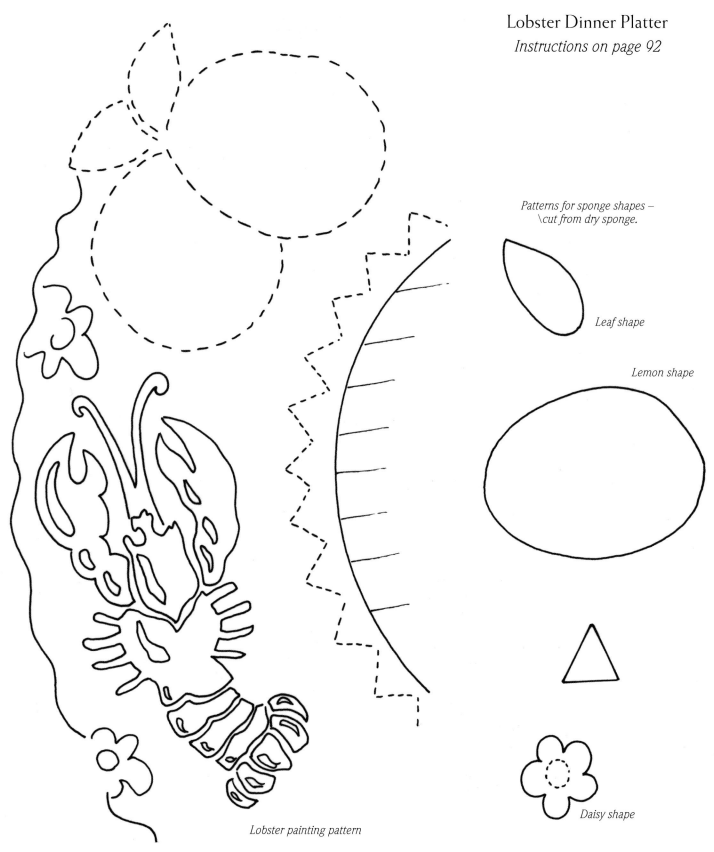

Lobster Dinner Platter
Instructions on page 92

Patterns for sponge shapes –
\cut from dry sponge.

Leaf shape

Lemon shape

Daisy shape

Lobster painting pattern

SERVING

IT

PRETTY

Serving dishes are some more items in our life that we want to be beautiful as well as functional – especially since they're often used to serve company. The domed cheese server project here will satisfy that desire, and you can proudly report that you painted it yourself. Transparent platters can be painted on the backside and safely used to serve food. (Do not paint surfaces that will come in contact with food, if the paints are not food safe.) Or, you can use a clear glass liner or a doiley liner atop the painted surface.

Platters can also be purely decorative, displayed on the walls or in easels. Choose glass or ceramic platters and adorn them with your own artistry.

Pictured right: Dome of Roses Cheese Server. See instructions on page 94.

Lobster Dinner

PLATTER

Designed by Patty Cox

YOU WILL NEED:

Oven-Bake Acrylic Enamel Paints:
(Food-Safe)
Dusty lavender
Light green
Light mustard
Purple
Red
Red-orange
Royal blue
Yellow

Item to Decorate:
White ceramic round platter, 13" diam.

Other Supplies:
Paint brushes: flat and liner
Sponge
Graphite transfer paper
Fine tip marker
Hole punch
Craft knife

See patterns on page 89.

HERE'S HOW:

1. TRANSFER PATTERNS: Use a small cereal bowl as a template. Draw a circle approximately 5-3/4" diameter in center of plate with fine tip pen. Transfer lobster pattern around edge of platter three times with graphite paper. Mark position of lemons (indicated by dotted lines on the lobster pattern). Freehand daisies with the fine tip marker, using one to three daisies between lemons and lobsters near edge of design. (A sample daisy pattern is given, but don't make them all exactly alike.)
2. CUT SPONGE SHAPES: Using lemon, leaf, and triangle patterns, cut these shapes from a dry sponge. Using a hole punch, punch a 1/4" diameter dot from dry sponge.
3. STRAIGHT LINES: Paint straight lines across center circle with light mustard, using the flat brush. Let dry.
4. LEMONS: Dip the lemon shaped sponge in yellow paint. Sponge yellow lemons in place on rim of platter. They are in sets of two; let one lemon slightly overlap the other in each set. Paint a red-orange shadow on one side of sponge. Also add a little light mustard to the sponge. Apply shadow on each lemon. Let dry.
5. LEAVES: Dip the leaf sponge into light green. Sponge two leaves onto each set of lemons, letting one overlap the other. Let dry.
6. When paint is dry, separate the two lemons and the two leaves in each set by scraping away paint between them with a craft knife. Refer to photo of project.
7. FLOWER CENTERS: Dip the 1/4" dot sponge in light mustard. Add a bit of red-orange to the sponge. Sponge flower centers in the center of each daisy area.
8. TRIANGLE BORDER: Dip triangle sponge in dusty lavender paint. Sponge triangle border around center circle, covering pen line.
9. LOBSTERS: Paint lobster sections with red. Paint highlight areas with red-orange.
10. Paint outer wavy-line border with red-orange, using a liner brush.
11. BACKGROUND: Squeeze royal blue and purple paint on a palette, but do not mix colors. Dip brush in both colors. Paint around designs on platter rim, leaving white space around each. Paint up to outline of daisy petals; the petals will remain the white of the platter.
12. When paint is thoroughly dry, remove any noticeable pen or transfer lines with a pencil eraser.
13. BAKE: Let dry for 48 hours. Then bake and cool in oven as directed in "Bake or Air Dry Projects." ⌒

Dome of Roses
CHEESE SERVER
Designed by Allison Stilwell

YOU WILL NEED:
Oven-Bake Acrylic Enamel Paints:
Green
Mustard
Navy
Red
White
Yellow

Item to Decorate:
Light colored marble round cheese slab
with glass dome

Other Supplies:
Paint brushes: #8 round, 3/4" flat shader,
and fine liner (#1 or smaller)

HERE'S HOW:
1. TOP SCALLOPS: Around the top knob of the dome, paint navy scallops with the round brush and a generous amount of paint. Make scallops approximately 3/4" wide. Let dry.
2. CHECKS: Decorate around the bottom of the dome with red checks every 1/2" or so. Use a 3/4" flat shader to make each stroke that represents one check. Let dry.
3. ROSES: Paint yellow circles evenly spaced around the curve or shoulder of the dome. Make them approximately 1" to 1-1/4" diameter. There are eight on project shown in the photo. Use a round brush and a generous amount of paint. This should be done with loose strokes to achieve a flower effect. Go back and add mustard strokes to indicate petals in the yellow circles.
4. VINES: Paint simple curving green lines between the yellow roses; use a fine liner brush. Paint a wavy line of green around outer edge of marble cheese slab. Add tiny leaves to the curving and wavy lines to make vines.
5. SMALL FLOWERS: Paint a border of small 5-petal flowers above the checks around bottom. Paint petals with navy. Make flowers approximately 1/2" wide. Add a dot of yellow for each flower center.
6. KNOB: Basecoat knob with red. Let dry. Add dots of white all over red knob, using the handle end of a brush.
7. BAKE: Let dry for 48 hours. Then bake and cool in oven as directed in "Bake or Air Dry Projects." ⌒

94

Spring Leaves
PLATTER
Designed by Allison Stilwell

YOU WILL NEED:
Oven-Bake Acrylic Enamel Paints:
(Food-Safe)

Avocado green   Brown   Dark green
Light Green   Medium green
Mustard   Sage green

Item to Decorate:
Large clear glass oblong platter, 14" x 18"

Other Supplies:
Various stamps of leaves: ivy, fern, and others
Paint brush: #6 shader   Cosmetic sponge

HERE'S HOW:

1. Sponge light green paint on entire rim of platter with the cosmetic sponge. Dab the paint on, working quickly and evenly. Let dry. Add a second coat. Let dry.
2. Stamp the various leaf patterns on the rim in a random manner, using all the different shades of green. Apply paint to the stamps with the cosmetic sponge, then stamp onto rim. Let dry.
3. Paint a checked border around the inside of the rim with the #6 shader brush. Alternate sage green and brown. Paint the checks of one color first, let dry, then paint the alternating checks with the other color.
4. Let dry for 48 hours. Then bake and cool in oven as directed in "Bake or Air Dry Projects." ⌒

CANISTERS

AND

CONTAINERS

Do we ever have enough containers? Most of us can always use more. They can be beautiful and unique, as well, by painting them yourself. Ceramic canisters, glass jars and bottles, and decorator boxes make wonderful accessories because they are not only decorative, they hold things!

Use them everywhere in the house. In the kitchen, they can hold flour and sugar, in the pantry they can hold special vinegars. Use them in the bath for bubble bath, bath oil, or toilet water. In the office, use decorator boxes for stamps or paper clips.

In glass, porcelain, or ceramic, you'll love painting these projects – for your own use or for special gift items.

Pictured right: Checkerboard 'n Ivy Canister Set. See instructions on page 110.

Pantry Beauty

VINEGAR BOTTLES

Designed by Allison Stilwell

CORNUCOPIA BOTTLE

YOU WILL NEED:

Oven-Bake Acrylic Enamel Paints:
Brown
Dark green
Light green
Mustard
Red
Violet
Yellow

Item to Decorate:
Green tinted decorative bottle (preferably with embossed cornucopia design), 11" tall

Other Supplies:
Paint brushes: round brushes, shader, fine liner (#1 or smaller)
Graphite paper (if bottle is not embossed)

HERE'S HOW:

1. This bottle had the design embossed on it. If yours does not, transfer the cornucopia design to opposite sides of the bottle with graphite paper. Both will be painted the same way.
2. Paint cornucopia with brown.
3. Fill your cornucopia with all kinds of fruit. Make little dots for grapes or cherries and larger dots for oranges or apples. Pears and lemons are basically dots, too, they just have an elongated end or ends. Paint lemons and banana with yellow, apples with red, grapes with violet, and peaches with mustard and touches of red. Paint leaves with dark green.
4. Paint 1/2" wide vertical stripes around top and bottom of bottle with light green.
5. Paint one or two cherries between stripes, painting cherries with red (dots), stems with brown, and leaf with dark green.
6. Let dry for 48 hours. Then bake and cool in oven as directed in "Bake or Air Dry Projects." ∿

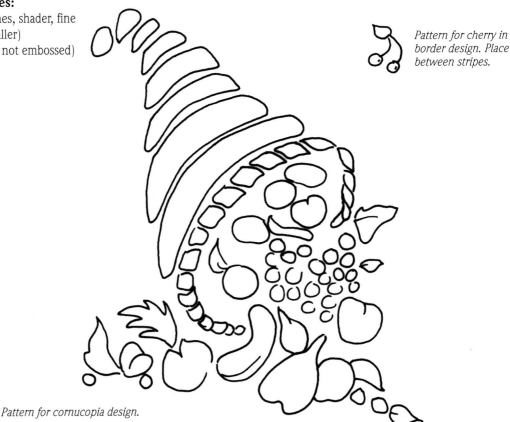

Pattern for cherry in border design. Place between stripes.

Pattern for cornucopia design.

FLOWER BASKET BOTTLE

YOU WILL NEED:

Oven-Bake Acrylic Enamel Paints:
Brown
Coral
Medium green
Dark blue
Dark green
Light blue
Light green
Mustard
Purple
Red
Terra cotta
Yellow

Item to Decorate:
Green tinted decorative bottle (preferably with embossed basket weave design at top and bottom), 11" tall

Other Supplies:
Paint brushes: round brushes, shader, fine liner (#1 or smaller)

HERE'S HOW:

1. BASKETRY: If you have embossed basket weave on your bottle, paint bottom "basketry" section with brown and highlight with terra cotta. If you do not, paint a plaid with terra cotta and add touches of brown for depth. A plaid is just lines of different widths and colors that intersect, so paint lines evenly spaced around bottle, then paint vertical lines across the horizontal lines. Keep adding lines until you are happy with the results.
2. FLOWERS: Above the basketry area, paint a variety of flowers with coral, red, mustard, light blue, dark blue, and purple. Fig. 1 shows a variety of simple flower shapes. Use coral and red for roses. Paint black eyed susans with mustard petals and brown centers. Paint blue bachelor buttons with mustard centers. Paint dot flowers with yellow centers. Paint leaves and stems with light, medium, and dark green.
3. Let dry for 48 hours. Then bake and cool in oven as directed in "Bake or Air Dry Projects." ⌒

Fig. 1

TOPIARY BOTTLE

YOU WILL NEED:

Oven-Bake Acrylic Enamel Paints:
Brown
Dark Green
Medium green
Terra cotta

Item to Decorate:
Green tinted decorative bottle, 11" tall

Other Supplies:
Paint brushes: round brushes, shader, fine liner (#1 or smaller)
Graphite transfer paper

HERE'S HOW:

1. Transfer pattern of topiaries around bottle right above bottom rim. They can also easily be freehanded. The pots are upside-down cones with the bottoms cut off and a line on the top. Or make a round pot by drawing a circle and putting a line on top so that it looks banded.
2. Paint pots with terra cotta. When dry add brown around the edges to add dimension.
3. Paint topiary shapes with medium green. Let dry. Paint dots all over them with dark green for leaves.
4. Paint stems and trunks with brown, using a liner brush.
5. Let dry for 48 hours. Then bake and cool in oven as directed in "Bake or Air Dry Projects." ⌒

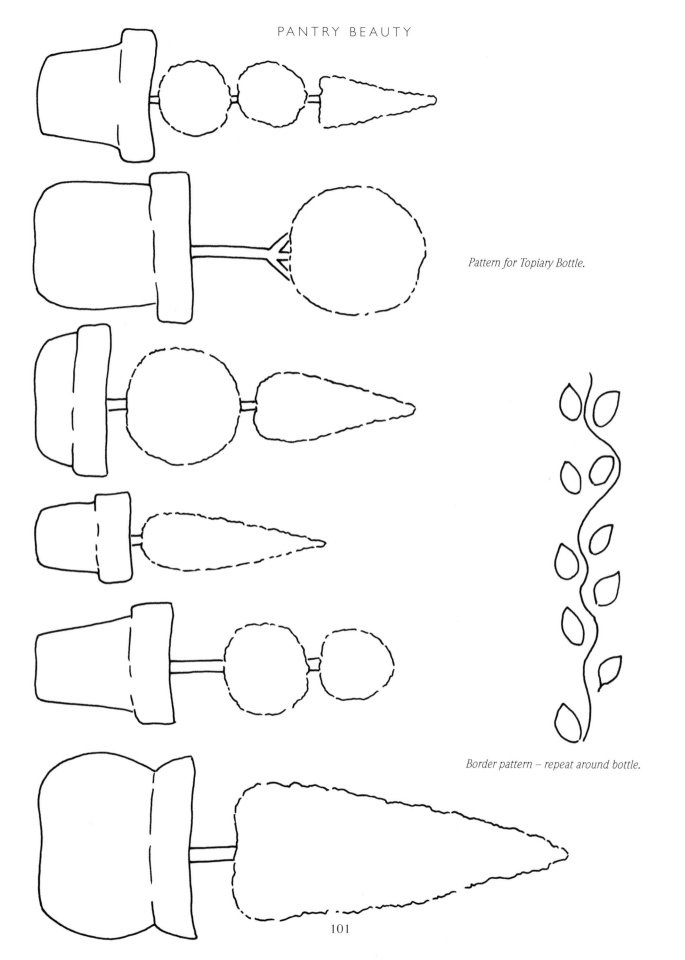

Pattern for Topiary Bottle.

Border pattern – repeat around bottle.

Personal Pleasures
TOILETRY BOTTLES
Designed by Gigi Smith-Burns

General Information for Painting Toiletry Bottles

These bottles are meant for decorative purposes and were painted with acrylic decorative paints. They cannot be washed in a dishwahser or with detergent. Simply wipe with a damp cloth when needed.

• PREPARATION

1. Wash bottle with vinegar and water to remove any oils that may be on the glass. Dry bottle.
2. Lightly mist bottle several times with matte finish acrylic spray; let dry after each coat.
3. Transfer pattern to bottle with graphite transfer paper.

• TERMINOLOGY & TECHNIQUES

Basecoat: The original solid application of main color. When basecoating, it will take several coats to make the basecoat appear opaque. Let dry after each coat.

Shade: Shading is used to darken or deepen an area. You may use several layers of shading, allowing each layer to stop short of the previous layer. The object of applying other layers of shading is to not obliterate the previous shading color but to lead your eye to the deepest area. Place shading where an object turns or goes under another object.

I use a 1/2" angle brush for most shading and highlighting. I use extender in my brush, but not a lot. Blot brush after dipping into the extender. Sideload the brush with paint unless otherwise indicated.

Highlight: Use to lighten or brighten an area. I sometimes use two highlights – the first with a duller yet light color and the second with a brighter color. Highlighting an area makes that area appear closer or brighter. Use the same brush and techniques as for shading.

Shimmer: Use a sideloaded flat brush which has been softened on the palette. Place the brush down and float color where the shimmer will be. Quickly reverse the process by flipping your brush over and floating color against the color that was just placed. This will make a shimmer effect with the outside fading out and the center of the shimmer the brightest.

Sideload: Load one side of a flat or angle brush. Do not allow paint to travel more than one-fourth of the way across the brush. Blend brush on wet palette.

Pivot Cheek Technique: This is not always used on a face. Some highlights are also accomplished in this manner. It is done with a flat or angle brush sideloaded with the color specified in Here's How:. With the color side on the inside, pivot the brush in a circle, keeping the water edge to the outside.

Pictured left to right: Rose Bouquet, Morning Glory, and Happy Days. See instructions on page 104.

Personal Pleasures
TOILETRY BOTTLES
Pictured on page 102-103

ROSE BOUQUET BOTTLE

YOU WILL NEED:

Acrylic Craft Paints:
Flesh
Grayish blue-violet
Green-black
Indigo
Light Green
Light yellow
Off-white
Wine

Item to Decorate:
Green tinted wave-shape bottle, 11" high

Other Supplies:
Paint brushes: 1/2" angle brush, #6/0
script liner, #4 and #12 flats
Stylus
Extender
Matte acrylic spray sealer
Matte spray varnish
Rose colored ribbon
Graphite transfer paper

HERE'S HOW:

Ribbon:
1. Basecoat with grayish blue-violet.
2. Shade with indigo.
3. Highlight with off-white + a touch of grayish blue-violet, using the shimmer technique.
4. Reinforce the previous shading with more indigo.
5. Paint lace with off-white, using a liner brush. Add dots to lace with off-white, using a stylus.

Rosebuds:
1. Basecoat with flesh.
2. Shade bottom and paint a "C" stroke on top of buds with wine. Let dry.
3. Highlight with an "S" stroke of off-white.
4. Paint stems with green-black.
5. Load liner brush with light green. Tip it into green-black. Stroke in the calyx and sepals around buds.

Leaves:
Load a #4 flat brush with light green. Sideload it with green-black. Stroke in leaves.

Finish:
1. Apply three or four coats of matte spray varnish. Let dry after each coat.
2. Tie rose ribbon around neck of bottle. ⌒

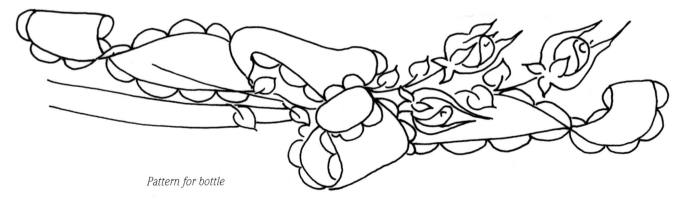

Pattern for bottle

HAPPY DAYS BOTTLE

YOU WILL NEED:

Acrylic Craft Paints:
Brick red
Brown
Dark green
Dark yellow
Green-black
Indigo
Light green
Light yellow
Off-white
Red-brown
Tan
Wine

Item to Decorate:
Cobalt blue triangular shaped bottle, 11" tall

Other Supplies:
Paint brushes: 1/2" angle brush, #6/0 script liner, #12 flat
Stylus
Extender
Matte acrylic spray
Matte spray varnish
White sheer ribbon
Graphite transfer paper

HERE'S HOW:

Clouds:
1. Sideload a 1/2" angle brush with off-white and fluff in clouds. Let dry.
2. Shade behind clouds with indigo.

Birdhouse on Right:
1. Basecoat with off-white.
2. Shade with indigo under roof and down left side. Paint stripes on birdhouse with indigo.
3. Paint opening with red-brown, making a dot with the handle end of brush. Make a red-brown dot with stylus for perch.
4. Basecoat roof with brick red.
5. Shade roof with wine at the tip and ends of roof.

Birdhouse on Left:
1. Basecoat with brick red.
2. Highlight center of house with a mix of tan + a touch of brick red. Let dry.
3. Shade under roof and down left side with wine. Paint stripes with wine + a touch of indigo.
4. Paint opening with red-brown, making a dot with the handle end of brush. Make a red-brown dot with stylus for perch.

Birdhouse Posts:
1. Basecoat with brown.
2. Shade with red-brown under house, at bottom, and down left side.

Sunflowers:
1. Basecoat with dark yellow. Basecoat center with red-brown.
2. Highlight center with little dots of light yellow on a "dirty" liner brush that had red-brown in it.

Filler Flowers:
1. Paint petals with off-white.
2. Paint centers with red-brown dots.

Leaves:
Load a #4 flat brush with light green. Sideload it with green-black. Stroke in leaves.

Foliage:
1. Corner load a #12 flat brush with light green. Stipple in foliage. Repeat with dark green, then with green-black. Let dry.
2. Corner load brush with brick red. Pick up some wine on the same corner. Dab in the flowers.
3. Randomly add dots of light yellow and of off-white to create interest in the foliage.

Finish:
1. Apply three or four coats of matte spray varnish. Let dry after each coat.
2. Tie white ribbon around neck of bottle. ⌒

Pattern for bottle

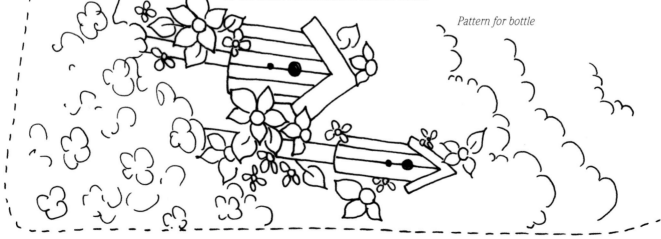

MORNING GLORY BOTTLE
Pictured on page 102

YOU WILL NEED:

Acrylic Craft Paints:

Dark green   Dark magenta
Flesh   Gray-plum
Green-black   Light green
Light yellow   Magenta
Off-white   Purple
Red-violet   Tan
Wine

Item to Decorate:

Green tinted square bottle, 3-1/2" square
x 9" tall

Other Supplies:

Paint brushes: 1/2" angle brush, #6/0
script liner, #4 and #12 flats
Extender
Matte acrylic spray
Matte spray varnish
Purple sheer ribbon
Graphite transfer paper

HERE'S HOW:

Refer to "Morning Glory Painting Worksheet" on page 107.

Leaves:
1. Basecoat with light green.
2. Shade base and down one side of center vein with dark green.
3. Highlight with light yellow.
4. Add tints of flesh.
5. Reinforce previous shading with green-black. Randomly reinforce shading on some leaves with green-black + wine.
6. Loosely outline leaves and add veins with green-black.

Top Flower:
1. Basecoat with gray-plum. Basecoat divisions between petals with off-white.
2. Shade outer edges and behind throat with red-violet. Shade outer edge of divisions with gray- plum.
3. Highlight throat area with tan. Let dry. Reinforce highlight with light yellow.

Middle Flower:
1. Basecoat with a half-and-half mix of grey-plum + magenta. Basecoat divisions between petals with off-white.
2. Shade outer edges and behind throat with dark magenta. Shade outer edge of divisions with the petal basecoat mix.
3. Highlight throat area with tan. Let dry. Reinforce highlight with light yellow.

Bottom Flower:
1. Basecoat with magenta. Basecoat divisions between petals with off-white.
2. Shade outer edges and behind throat with purple. Shade outer edge of divisions with magenta.
3. Highlight throat area with tan. Let dry. Reinforce highlight with light yellow.

Filler Flowers:
1. Paint petals with off-white.
2. Make dots of light yellow for centers.

Filler Leaves:
Load a #4 flat brush with light green. Sideload it with green-black. Stroke in leaves.

Finish:
1. Apply three or four coats of matte spray varnish. Let dry after each coat.
2. Tie purple ribbon around neck of bottle. ⌒

Pattern for bottle

Morning Glory Worksheet

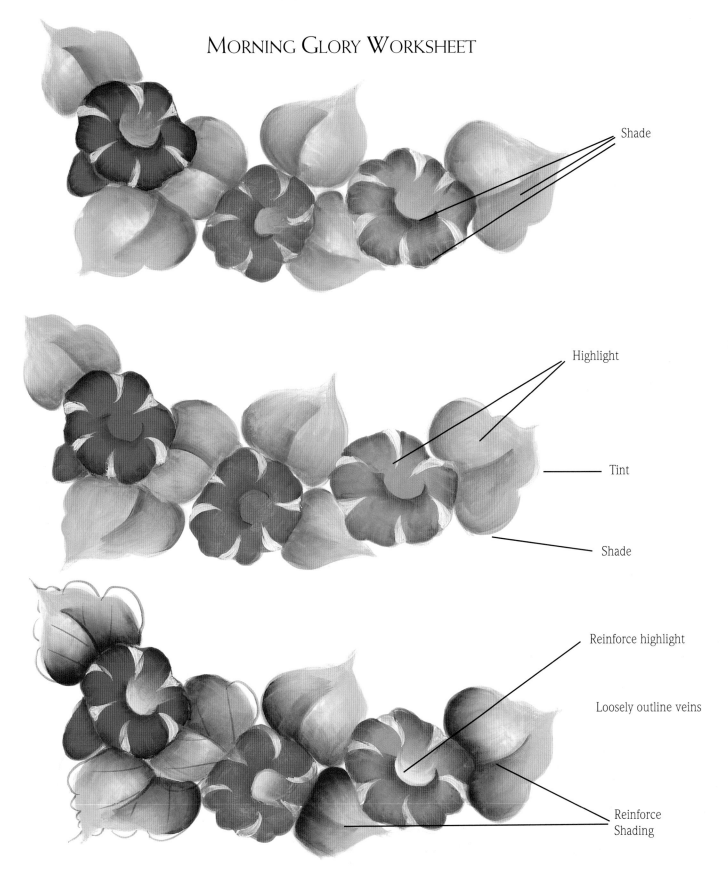

Shade

Highlight

Tint

Shade

Reinforce highlight

Loosely outline veins

Reinforce Shading

Hearts & Cherries
LIMOGES-STYLE BOXES
Designed by Patty Cox
PATCHWORK HEART

YOU WILL NEED:
Acrylic Craft Paints:
Aqua
Flesh
Light green
Red
Medium yellow
Orange
Royal blue

Item to Decorate:
Heart shaped resin box with lid, 3" x 2-1/3" x 1-1/2" high

Other Supplies:
Paint brushes: flat and liner
Clear acrylic sealer
Graphite transfer paper

HERE'S HOW:
1. Transfer patterns to lid and sides of box. Start pattern for sides at point of box.
2. Paint background of roses sections on lid and sides with medium yellow.
3. Paint background of leaves section on lid with a wash of royal blue.
4. Paint roses with flesh. Highlight with medium yellow and orange. Outline with red. Paint stripes in the rose section on sides of box with the rose colors.
5. Paint all leaves with light green + medium yellow. Outline leaves and add vein lines with royal blue + aqua.
6. In upper left section of lid, paint wider wavy lines with aqua and narrow wavy lines with royal blue. Paint between wavy lines with light green + yellow. Add orange dots on aqua stripes.
7. On box, in section below lid section in step 6, paint stripe with aqua. Paint leaves as in step 5. Paint background between stripes and around leaves with light green + yellow.
8. On box at left of heart point, paint dots with aqua. Paint around dots with a wash of royal blue, leaving some white showing around dots. Add royal blue lines on background and curves on dots.
9. On box at right of heart point, alternate stripes of a royal blue wash and light green + yellow. Add accent lines of royal blue.

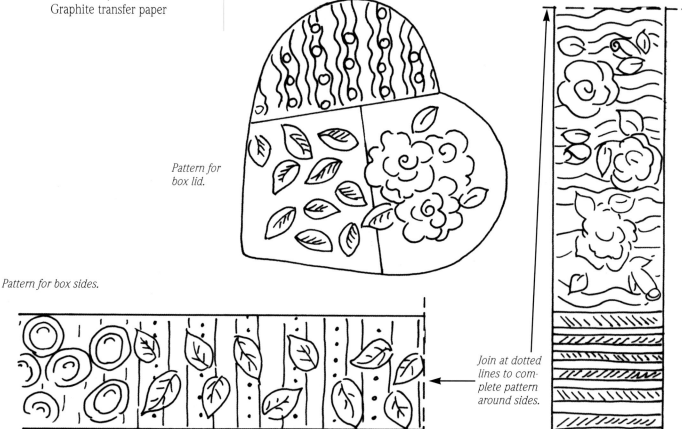

Pattern for box lid.

Pattern for box sides.

Join at dotted lines to complete pattern around sides.

CHERRY BASKET

YOU WILL NEED:

Acrylic Craft Paints:
Black   Dark green   Ivory
Light green   Red   Sunflower yellow

Item to Decorate:
Round resin box with lid, 2-3/4" diam. x 1-1/2" high

Other Supplies:
Paint brushes: flat and liner
Red flat-back marble
Light oak antiquing stain (optional)
Antique decoupage finish
Epoxy glue
Graphite transfer paper

HERE'S HOW:

1. Basecoat box with sunflower yellow. Let dry.
2. Paint edging on box and box lid with ivory. Let dry. Paint black stripes around edging on box and lid approximately every 1/2".
3. Transfer leaf pattern to lid. Transfer cherry pattern four times around sides of box.
4. Paint leaves with light green. Outline and add center vein lines with dark green.
5. Paint cherries with red. Paint cherry stems with dark green.
6. Make black dots on background in an all-over pattern around cherries and leaves on box sides and lid. Use the handle end of a brush to make dots.
7. Optional: When paint has dried, paint antiquing stain over box. Wipe away stain with a cloth. Let dry.
8. Coat box with antique decoupage finish. Let dry.
9. Glue marble in center of lid with epoxy glue. ~

Lid

Sides

Checkerboard 'n Ivy
CANISTER SET
Designed by Patty Cox

YOU WILL NEED:

Oven-Bake Acrylic Enamel Paints:
Dark green
Green
Light green
Lilac
Pale yellow
Purple
Red-orange
White
Yellow

Item to Decorate:
White ceramic canister set

Other Supplies:
Paint brushes: flat and liner
Sponges
Ivy border stencil, 1" high
Violet crayon
Hole punch

HERE'S HOW:

1. Stencil ivy pattern around base of each canister and around knobs on lid with green; shade leaves with dark green. Stencil by pouncing paint on a sponge into open areas of stencil.

2. Draw two vertical lines about 2" apart on side of each canister with crayon. End lines at the ivy border.

3. Cut two 3/4" squares from a dry sponge. Moisten them with a little water to make them soft.; remove excess water. Dip one square in pale yellow and the other in light green. Sponge a checkerboard pattern with these two colors around canister, leaving 1/8" between squares. Leave space between the two crayon lines unpainted.

4. Cut a 1/4" wide strip of sponge. Dip into lilac paint. Sponge a 1/4" vertical stripe along the right crayon line. Skip 3/8", moving to the left and sponge a very narrow vertical line

with lilac for the left side of daisy section. Use the side of the sponge, if necessary. Draw three daisy shapes with the crayon to the left of this sponged line as shown in Fig. 1. Sponge around the daisies with lavender creating a 1" wide sponged stripe that contains the white daisies.

5. Place lid on canister. Draw a wedge on lid top with the crayon, aligning width of the wedge with width of the sponged stripes on canister side. Sponge the narrow side of the wedge with lilac, as if the 1/4" stripe on side continues on lid. Draw two daisies, using the crayon, in the wider area to be sponged. Sponge around the daisies as before.

6. Paint a purple vertical line between the lilac sponged stripes on canister side and on lid, using a liner brush.

7. Paint white daisies with five or six petals (as in Fig. 1) on some of the green sponged squares of the checkerboard. Let dry.

8. Punch a dot from a sponge, using a hole punch. Dip this into yellow paint. Add a little red-orange on the side of it. Stamp centers of all daisies with this sponge dot.

9. Dip the handle end of a paint brush in lilac paint. Dip one side of it in purple. Make dots around ivy on bottom and on lid.

10. When paint is dry, remove all noticeable crayon lines.

11. Let dry for 48 hours. Then bake and cool in oven as directed in "Bake or Air Dry Projects." ∽

METRIC CONVERSION CHART

INCHES TO MILLIMETERS AND CENTIMETERS

Inches	MM	CM	Inches	MM	CM
1/8	3	.3	4	102	10.2
1/4	6	.6	5	127	12.7
3/8	10	1.0	6	152	15.2
1/2	13	1.3	7	178	17.8
5/8	16	1.6	8	203	20.3
3/4	19	1.9	9	229	22.9
7/8	22	2.2	10	254	25.4
1	25	2.5	11	279	27.9
1-1/4	32	3.2	12	305	30.5
1-1/2	38	3.8			
1-3/4	44	4.4			
2	51	5.1			
2-1/2	64	6.4			
3	76	7.6			
3-1/2	89	8.9			

YARDS TO METERS

Yards	Meters
1/8	.11
1/4	.23
3/8	.34
1/2	.46
5/8	.57
3/4	.69
7/8	.80
1	.91
1-1/2	1.37
1-5/8	1.49
1-3/4	1.60
1-7/8	1.71
2	1.83
2-1/2	2.29
3	2.74
4	3.66
5	4.57
6	5.49
7	6.40
8	7.32
9	8.23
10	9.14

INDEX

Continued on page 112

INDEX